I dedicate this book to
Nancy Wardle
She is on the front and back cover
She is my Alpha and Omega
And the love of my life
W.A.L.K
(With A Loving Kiss)
Martin

Special acknowledgement to Bev Mason

Without Bev this book might never have happened. She has kept the project going from its inception to its completion. Bev is the role model for the content of the book, she walks, she jogs, she swims and she Curves and works all day sitting on an exercise ball. When you call the Speakwell office it's Bev's, always cheerful, voice that will greet you and help you.

**Walking, Weight and Wellness**

# Walking, Weight and Wellness

## Your Pedometer Resource Guide

Dr. Martin Collis

Walking, Weight and Wellness
Published in 2006 by Trafford Publishing,
Victoria, BC, Canada

Cover design: Johanna St. Michael, BFA
Decodent Dezigns, www.decodezigns.com
Interior book design and typeset: Bev Mason, Speakwell

Cover photography: Johanna St. Michael, BFA
All exercise photography Johanna St. Michael

Photograph of Dr. Collis on bio page 346 Mark MacDonald,
Business Vancouver Island, www.businessvi.ca

Note for Librarians: A cataloguing record for this book is available from Library and Archives
Canada at www.collectionscanada.ca/amicus/index-e.html
ISBN 1-4251-0180-1

*Offices in Canada, USA, Ireland and UK*

**Book sales for North America and international:**
Trafford Publishing, 6E–2333 Government St.,
Victoria, BC  V8T 4P4  CANADA
phone 250 383 6864 (toll-free 1 888 232 4444)
fax 250 383 6804; email to orders@trafford.com
**Book sales in Europe:**
Trafford Publishing (UK) Limited, 9 Park End Street, 2nd Floor
Oxford, UK  OX1 1HH  UNITED KINGDOM
phone +44 (0)1865 722 113 (local rate 0845 230 9601)
facsimile +44 (0)1865 722 868; info.uk@trafford.com
**Order online at:**
trafford.com/06-1937

10 9 8 7 6 5 4 3 2

Disclaimer
Serious diseases should always be treated under medical supervision.
The material in this book is for educational purposes only and is not intended for use in
diagnosing or treating any individual.

# Walking, Weight and Wellness

*However many words you read,*
*what good will they do*
*if you do not act upon them?*

The Dhammapada

*The Path of Wisdom* 200BC

*Some people want an hour of your time,*
*I want a piece of the rest of your life.*

Martin Collis

# Preface

Welcome – which breaks down to 'come in wellness', there's no better way. In the words of Cicero I want, *to teach, to stir the mind and to provide enjoyment*. But I want more, I want your feet on the street, the trails or the treadmill, I want you eating well and I want you feeling great. This book is a call to action and your actions will be the measure of its success.

The left hand pages of this book bring you wisdom, humor, stories, quotations, poems and inspiration and the right hand pages help you channel that inspiration into positive, life-changing programs. (If it doesn't confuse you too much, the left hand pages are for your right brain, and the right hand pages are for your left brain). I acknowledge all the great thinkers, scholars and researchers, who bring the book depth and authenticity, but I have chosen not to fill the back pages with lists of formal references, they're all available on the Internet. Likewise, there are no academic footnotes, although surely a book about walking is one big footnote. In Alice in Wonderland there's a scene in which Alice asks the Cheshire Cat for directions.

Alice: *Which road should I take?*

*The journey of a thousand miles must begin with a single step.*

Lao-Tse

*Fitness can contribute as much to the Nation's health as immunization and sanitation advances have done in the past.*

R. Egeborg, M.D.
Special assistant to US
Secretary for Health Policy

Cheshire Cat: *Where are you going?*
Alice: *I don't know.*
Cheshire Cat: *Then it doesn't matter.*

The following pages are filled with information to help you chose a way that's right for you and unique programs to get you there. You'll discover 'The Power of Fifteen', 'Circle Canada' and 'Route 66', you'll find out the truth about walking, weight-loss and weight-control and why walking and lifestyle programs belong everywhere, from schools to the workplace, from seniors' centers to city streets.

I pay special attention to the pedometer, an inexpensive little device, which can transform your walking program and play a big part in getting you where you need to go. You will be challenged and at times you might fall short, but that only sweetens the joy of your success, and to miss the joy is to miss it all.

One of my favorite authors, John Griffin, said, *Write nothing you do not feel and believe to be true.* That I've done, you have my word.

**Note**: Throughout the book quotations are shown in italics as in the John Griffin quotation shown above.

*Talking about my baby,*
*He's a walking miracle.*

The Essex, 1963

*People usually consider walking on water or in*
*thin air a miracle. But I think the real miracle is*
*not to walk either on water or in thin air, but to*
*walk on the earth. Every day we are engaged in a*
*miracle, which we don't even realize.*

Thich Nhat Hanh

# Introduction

## You're a Walking Miracle

I want you to look good and feel great,
I want you to be all that you can be,
I want you to walk.

'Walking, Weight and Wellness' provides a roadmap, which will guide you to high-level wellness. It will put back the movement in your life that our culture has stolen away. It will provide a formula to be slim and firm in a land where it has become 'normal' to be fat and flabby. It will provide islands of calm in a world of noise and distraction.

We are vigorous, active animals that do well when we move and badly when we are sedentary. The movement which comes naturally to humans is walking, and I want you to walk nearly every day. We are born with a 100-year warranty but we have to read the small print. The small print tells us to move on a daily basis; the small print says, *walk*.

I titled the introduction *You're a Walking Miracle* not in any religious sense, but to remind you of the extraordinary nature of the human body/mind and what it can accomplish. The word 'miracle' comes from the Latin 'miraculum', meaning, *object of wonder* and to anyone who looks

> *If God had wanted us to walk*
> *He'd have given us two legs*
> *and made us to stand erect.*

> Anonymous

---

G.O.L.F. – Getting Old, Lazy and Fat

The game of golf has become a metaphor for life in North America. On the majority of courses the game is all about money and convenience. 90% of Floridian golfers now use powered golf carts, many of which have GPS systems so that they can be tracked to deliver beer, chips and hotdogs to the riders. Many courses actually charge a fee of $5 to $15 for walking the course.

The August 2000 issue of the American Journal of Medicine published a Finnish study in which 55 golfers in the 48 – 64 year old age range agreed to golf for 20 weeks with a minimum of 2 rounds a week, always walking the course. In 20 weeks they averaged a weight loss of 1.2kg (2.64lbs), lost 2.2cm (1 inch) from their waists and improved their cardiovascular fitness.

A reader to my online newsletter, 'Well', who was an admittedly poor golfer, recorded 9000 steps for a 9-hole round of golf and a whopping 19000 steps for 18 holes. The totals on her pedometer were much more important than those on her scorecard.

---

carefully at the human body/mind surely they see an *object of wonder*. It is a vast complex of trillions of interconnected cells. There are at least 10 times as many cells in our bodies as there are stars in the Milky Way. Marcel Proust reminded us that a sense of wonder comes not just from discovering new things and places, but by looking at familiar things through **new eyes**. I want you to look with new eyes at walking and its transformative powers. I want you to see yourself as a *walking miracle*.

**Technical note:**

What are we using, meters or miles?
Imperial measures or metric?
Two different countries, two different styles,
No need to get stressed or dyspeptic.

As this book will be read throughout North America and beyond, I have used both metric and Imperial measures in the text. I often include both, but in some cases, where it seems appropriate, write only in terms of miles or kilometers, pounds or kilograms, and inches or centimeters. If you need to convert one measurement system to another you can go to http://www.metric-conversions.org/measurement-conversions.htm

*Silvio, silver and gold can't buy back the beat of a heart grown cold.*

Bob Dylan

*It used to be said that you're too old to exercise. Well, the truth is that you're too old not to exercise. Most of what passes as aging really isn't — it's disuse.*

Walter Bartz

# 1

# Walking Can Save Your Life

Walking can save your life; it's as simple as that.

When I was writing a book for the Canadian Federal Government on *Employee Fitness*, I interviewed a high-ranking administrator in the Post Office. I've never forgotten what she said, *The letter carriers are ruining the superannuation (pension) fund, they're living too long.* The men and women who walked each day to deliver the mail were living longer and better than the insurance tables predicted.

I recently put a pedometer on our letter carrier and on a slightly shortened route he walked 18,598 steps. He has no problem maintaining his weight or keeping fit except when he takes a sedentary holiday.

Information from the long-term Framingham Study notes that you will gain one extra year of life for each mile (approximately 2000 steps) you average on a daily basis, up to 5 miles a day. So that someone who walks an average of 5 miles per day (10,000 steps) can expect 5 more quality years than their sedentary contemporaries.

*The goal in life is to die young as late as possible.*

Ashley Montagu

*When things are bad what a person needs is not a new philosophy but a new regimen - a different diet, or more exercise.*

Bertrand Russell

Study after study after study have proved that walking and other forms of exercise promote the kind of health benefits that will literally save your life. If there were a pill or product that delivered the benefits of walking everybody would want it. Just imagine a pill that:

Improved   -muscle tone
        -bone strength
        -memory
        -immune function
        -HDLs (the good cholesterol)
        -sexual performance
        -sleep
        -eye-sight
        -healing
        -self-esteem

while lowering -blood pressure
        -stress
        -LDL's (the bad cholesterol)
        -and, of course, weight.

This same pill would prevent, cure or control diabetes, heart disease, hypertension, Alzheimer's, stroke, many forms of cancer, depression, osteo-arthritis, obesity and the disease states associated with it. Of course, there are side effects, such as joie-de-vivre, delayed aging and an improved quality and length of life.

Such a pill would outsell any product on the market, but because it's free and doesn't come in a packet or pill bottle we devalue it. Instead of looking for opportunities to walk we avoid or ignore them and have endless reasons not to take a step in the right direction. The avoidance phrases roll easily off the tongue.

"Not today."
"I'd miss the big game."
"I'm too busy."
"It's raining."
"I'm not up to it."

*Did she get tired or did she just get lazy?*
Don Henley and Glenn Frey of *The Eagles*
From the song *Lying Eyes*

*If you want to know if your brain is flabby,*
*feel your legs.*

Bruce Barton

*Here lies, extinguished in his prime,*
*A victim of modernity.*
*Yesterday he hadn't time*
*And now he has eternity.*

Piet Hein

"I'm tired."
"I've got to drive the kids."
"I'd miss 'American Idol'."
"I've got too much paperwork."
"I'll do it later."

Of course you never *do it later* because you run out of time.

I could fill this book with studies about the benefits of walking but it might not change your behavior. A wise old friend, George Sheehan, told me, *people don't do things just because it's good for them, there has to be some pleasure.*

There's plenty of pleasure in a walk, which can be social or solitary, vigorous or easy, early or late and can take place almost any time, any place any where. In the movement of walking you discover stillness and problems get smaller with each step, ideas fill your brain, stress recedes as you align your body/mind and step-by-step your spirit is restored.

> Before you read more, turn information into action and take a walk. Maybe just go round the block or park, around the corridors of your hotel or up and down your apartment stairs. Try counting your steps and see how long it takes you to do 1000..

*Be first a good animal.*

Emerson

*The moment my legs begin to move,
my thoughts begin to flow.*

Henry David Thoreau

# 2

# Why Walking is the Most Popular Form of Exercise in North America

I've been asked, *Why write a book on walking? Why not write about swimming, jogging, strength training, biking, yoga and all the other many splendored forms of physical activity?* There is a reason. All these forms of exercise are wonderful and can enhance cardiovascular conditioning, improve flexibility and bone strength, help you lose weight or control weight and contribute to happiness and health, **if you do them on a regular basis**. I repeat, there are many benefits from many forms of physical activity **if you do them on a regular basis**. But so many activities die a logistical death. I've known people who set out to swim their way to weight loss and fitness, only to be frustrated by crowded pools, over chlorination, leaky goggles, colds, lost ear plugs, wet hair and numerous facility problems ranging from parking and scheduling to less than perfect hygiene in the showers. Incidentally, it's not easy to lose weight swimming. In the late 60s I coached many world-record holders in swimming; our swimmers would typically work out 4 hours a day and even doing that volume of work some of our teenage women had to be careful of their diet so as not to gain weight.

Cross-country skiing burns a bundle of calories **but you do need skis, boots and other clothing**, you might need to drive out to the trails and you

*The sum of the whole is this:*
*walk and be happy:*
*walk and be healthy.*
*The best way to lengthen out our days*
*is to walk steadily and with purpose.*

Charles Dickens

also need snow, which isn't always around. Water skiing needs water, a boat and driver, skis, and a bunch of safety equipment.

Any activity, which needs a special facility, such as a gym, rink, studio, dojo, or court means than many well-intentioned people will find reasons not to go. Part of the fitness 'industry' is based on the fact that people have good intentions, make commitments and pay money, but are unable or unwilling to follow through. Every fitness club or studio relies on the fact that the majority of people who sign up as members rarely or never show up. If everyone made use of their memberships, the gyms and studios would be overrun.

The dusty bike with a flat tire in the garage doesn't help you burn calories, nor does the rowing machine which *conveniently folds up to go under your bed*, where it often stays.

The reason I say walking is the best exercise and the one that burns most calories **is because we can do it**. We **can** walk to work, walk to the store, walk the stairs between floors, walk at lunchtime, walk morning, noon and night. We are designed to walk and feel good when we walk. With the right clothing there is little the weather can do to curtail outdoor walking, even if it might mean strapping on some snow shoes or putting on some rain gear. In extreme climates a number of people take part in mall walking programs to escape the Southern heat or Northern cold

Walking is do-able, you already know how to walk, walking's free, walking can be the core around which you build your eating and activity lifestyle. Walking burns calories, clears your head, improves your posture, assists the circulation and saves your life. We've known all this for thousands of years, there's a Latin phrase that says it all.

## *Solvitur Ambulando*

- Walking solves all things

*We are not statues; we're slow moving cellular fountains, replacing over 90% of our cells every year. We can recreate ourselves in a matter of months.*

Martin Collis

*What lies beyond us and what lies before us are tiny matters when compared with what lies within us.*

Ralph Waldo Emerson

# 3

# What Research Tells us About Walking and Wellness

I can summarize the research in two words. Walking works. If you are not convinced about the benefits of walking I will offer you a challenge. Find **one major study** in which subjects were on a consistent walking program and **showed no health benefits**. I don't believe such a study exists.

I'm not going to list hundreds of references, which have catalogued the benefits of walking. I'll mention some of the major studies but it's not reading research that will convince you, it's putting on your walking shoes and discovering the benefits for yourself.

Exercise epidemiologists Dr. Ralph Paffenbarger and Dr. Steven Blair know as much about the effects of physical activity on our lives as anyone in North America. In one major study they have followed 17,000 male Harvard graduates for over 40 years and established a clear relationship between their activity levels and their rates of mortality (death) from all chronic diseases. Paffenbarger and Blair looked at all physical activity, but Robert Sweetgall of Creative Walking Inc. [www.creativewalking.com/] translated their weekly activity calories into daily steps and came up with the following graph, which correlated mortality (death) with physical activity patterns.

# Let's Take a Walk

### (With apologies to Cole Porter)

*Cats do it, dogs do it,*
*Netherlanders in their clogs do it.*
*Let's do it, lets take a walk.*

*Some bike it, but don't like it.*
*They would rather wear their boots and hike it.*
*Let's do it, let's take a walk.*

*Dickens did it, Gandhi did it,*
*Thomas Jefferson, too.*
*Hippocrates in ancient Greece did it*
*And now it's time for you.*

*Put on your ped and do it, get off your bed and do it.*
*Don't turn on the tube and say, 'Oh screw it'.*
*Let's do it. Let's just take a walk.*

Lyrics by Martin Collis

*Genetics loads the gun, but lifestyle fires it off.*

Unknown

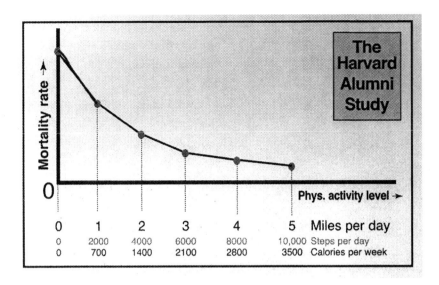

Clearly the biggest improvement is between doing nothing and walking a mile a day (1.6km). But there are big improvements between a mile a day (1.6km) and two miles a day (3.2km) and continued improvements when you get up to 3 miles (4.8km/6000 steps). After this there are diminishing longevity returns from walking further, although there are plenty of positive benefits from a long hike, not the least of which is the mental stimulation. As William James once said, *The length of my walking is the length of my writing.*

### Don't Blame Your Genes

We can't cut down the family tree and we can't pick our parents, but we can make the best of the genetic cards we are dealt. Genes mostly make suggestions, they might 'suggest' that we lead a sedentary life or 'suggest' that we put on some weight, but they are merely 'suggestions' and not demands and we can re-educate ourselves to be active and slim. A study in Finland looked at 16,000 men and women from the National Registry of Twins. The Journal of the American Medical Association reported that the twins who walked regularly cut their risk of premature death by 44% when compared with their sedentary siblings.

*The average Canadian should be getting
10,000 steps a day.*

Ruth Collins-Nakai
Former President of the
Canadian Medical Association

*A five mile walk (about 10,000 steps) will do
more good for an unhappy but otherwise healthy
adult than all the medicine and psychology in the
world.*

Paul Dudley White
Former Surgeon General

## It's Unanimous, Walking is Good for You

It's hard to get experts to agree on anything, but there are no dissenting voices about the value of walking, although there is still some discussion about how much is optimal. The Surgeon General's suggestion for a number of years has been 1/2 hour a day (about 1/50$^{th}$ of your life), but recently that suggestion is being doubled to an hour a day by a number of health agencies.

In a 2004 release summarizing the benefits of exercise, and particularly walking, the Harvard School of Public Health said,

*Brisk walking fills the bill for moderate intensity activity. How fast is brisk? For the average person it means walking 3-4 miles (4.8 to 6.4km) an hour, or about as fast as you'd walk if you were late for an important appointment. Walking is an ideal exercise for many people – it doesn't require any special equipment, it can be done any time and any place, and is generally very safe.*

*Major studies such as the Nurses' Health Study, Health Professionals Follow-Up Study, Women's Health Study, Women's Health Initiative, the Honolulu Heart Program and many others have demonstrated that this simple form of exercise substantially reduces the chances of developing heart disease, stroke and diabetes in a variety of populations.*

Walking is wonderful, it's good for your legs and lungs, heart and head, it will help you live longer, love better and lighten-up in more ways than one.

*The only way we are going to improve is if we actually get out there and get better.*

Jason Bay

(Pittsburgh Pirates)

Thomas Jefferson acquired an early pedometer in France and brought it back to the US. Jefferson became a committed step counter and it's not surprising that his quotations are featured in this book.

*The sovereign invigorator of the body is exercise and of all exercise walking is the best.*

Thomas Jefferson

# 4

# Pedometer Walking

*Every step you take I'll be watching you.*
Sting

## Introduction to Pedometers

Walking is a foundation of wellness and the most useful piece of equipment to enhance your walking experience is the pedometer. The basic pedometer will count your steps, while more sophisticated models will calculate calories burned, distance covered and even play little tunes and give spoken messages.

Pedometers are not new and the remarkable mind of Leonardo DaVinci designed a prototype. The concept of step counting really came of age in Japan in the 60's, where pedometers still sell in multiple millions each year.. Pedometers help you with goal setting, recording and understanding what it takes to burn calories. They will help you discover sensible solutions to the senseless spiral of overeating and under exercising. Walking can transform your life and pedometers will get you walking

Research by Hultquist et al. compared female subjects, whose target was 10,000 steps a day, with another matched group whose target was to walk 30 minutes a day. On days they completed their 30-minute walk, the 30-minute group averaged 9505 steps and on days they didn't do their 30-minute walk, the average was 5597 steps. The 10,000-step group averaged

*It is difficult to say what is impossible, for the dream of yesterday is the hope of today and the reality of tomorrow.*

Bob Goddard

*When you take charge of your life there is no need to ask permission of other people or society at large. When you ask permission you give someone power over your life.*

Geoffrey F. Abert

11,775 on days they did a purposeful walk and 7780 when they didn't.

What I draw from these results is that:
(I)   Any goal helps people increase their walking, and
(II)  A target number of steps (e.g. 10,000) is more effective in getting people to increase their walking than a time target.

The 10,000-step group averaged over 2,000 steps a day more than the 30-minute group. At 20 steps per calorie that's 100 calories a day difference. Now multiply that 100 calories by 365 to see what difference these extra 2000 steps a day would make in a year.

365 days x 100 calories = 36,500 calories burned

There are 3500 calories in one pound and about 7700 in a kilogram. So that in one year the 10,000-step group would burn an extra 10lbs worth of weight (or nearly 5kg).

### Why Use a Pedometer?

*What gets measured gets done.*
Tom Peters

A good pedometer will record every step of your comings and goings, your trips to the kitchen, your movement around the office and, more importantly, the steps you take when you go outside into the 'real' world and walk to the store or take a life-saving purposeful walk.

Why do we need a pedometer to record our steps? Because without it we would be guessing and people almost always exaggerate the amount of walking and exercise they 'remember' doing and conveniently forget many of the calories they consume. When I spoke with a researcher who was doing a telephone survey about exercise, his comments were that, *everybody lies* and that people have *an amazing ability to kid themselves.*

If we want to get fit, if we want to lose weight and if we want to be all that we can be, we have to get real. Getting real can mean keeping track of your daily steps, understanding the relationship between the steps you take

*The problem is not that your hopes (goals)
are too high and you fail to reach them,
it's that they're too low and you do!*

Michelangelo

and the calories you burn and, if you are concerned about your weight, monitoring your food intake and using an accurate scale.

I'm a believer in wearing my pedometer every waking minute; it goes on my belt when I get dressed in the morning and comes off when I go to bed at night. This means I'll be credited with some little shuffle steps and maybe a few *steps* for getting up and down from a chair, but it balances out because extra effort steps such as stair climbing or carrying a heavy load are still recorded the same as regular walking steps.

This is not a precise science, but it is a very good picture of your daily activity level and that's what you need.

### 10,000 Steps a Day

Why 10,000 steps? Why not 9,000 or 11,000 steps a day? The answer is that there is nothing magic about the number 10,000, but that it is a great goal for health maintenance. We imported the concept of 10,000 steps from Japan, where the term *Manpo-Kei,* which literally means *10,000 steps meter*, was a mantra for many of their walking clubs. Dr. Y. Hatano of Kyushu University reports that over seven million manpo-keis (pedometers) are sold every year in Japan. North America has imported the concept of 10,000 steps a day from Japan and has exported the idea of fast food and in terms of health, certainly got the better of that exchange.

In speaking with a number of academics and health professionals I am told that 10,000 steps a day is too much for the average Canadian and American. In her book, *Manpo-Kei,* Dr. Tudor-Locke reports a study in which 730 middle-aged workers participated in a 10,000 steps-a-day program, but only 83 of the 730 stayed with the program for the full 12 weeks. To me this highlights the importance of creating supportive groups and programs, such as Circle Canada, Route 66 and The Power of Fifteen to keep people focused on their goal.

Active young children should be doing more than 10,000 steps, while age, arthritis and chronic disease will make a target of less than 10,000 steps realistic for some older adults. But this still leaves tens of millions of adults for whom 10,000 steps a day is a challenging and attainable goal.

*Unhappy business men/women would increase their happiness more by walking 6 miles a day than any conceivable change in philosophy.*

Bertrand Russell

I say 'amen' to that, but the good news is that they don't have to walk 6 miles. Three miles of purposeful walking provides a powerful positive stimulus and walks of 2 miles or one mile provide many, many positive, measurable benefits.

Yes, 10,000 steps might mean getting up early to walk before it's too hot. 10,000 steps could involve coats, hats, scarves and boots because of the cold. You might have to get your steps indoors on a treadmill. It might be inconvenient and yes, you will have to be creative to stay with that non-negotiable 10,000 steps a day that you have promised yourself. But the pay-offs are so great that once you establish the 10,000 a day habit, it will become a part of you and a part of your day that you'll want to add to rather than relinquish. In the words of the legendary Johnny Kelly, who completed 61 Boston marathons, including 2 wins, and died recently at 97, *Every day I can't go out on the road, I feel that something's been stolen from me.* That's how you'll come to feel when deprived of your walk.

The researchers and academics (of which I am one) are doing study after study to "prove" the value of 10,000 steps a day. But after 30 years studying exercise and health I would stake my life on the following statement. *If the people of North America averaged 10,000 steps a day, we would see a huge improvement in physical health, mental health, happiness and almost any positive statistic you could measure and we would save multiple billions of dollars in health care.*

## 10,000 Steps A Day is a S.M.A.R.T. Goal

A useful acronym for successful goal setting is SMART (Specific, Measurable, Agreeable, Realistic and Time-limited).

**Specific –**   10,000 steps, no less (or whatever number you designate).

**Measurable** – No problem, your pedometer will record every step.

**Agreeable–** Walking is the most popular and one of the most pleasant forms of exercise in North America.

**Realistic -**   10,000 steps is easily attainable by most healthy adults. The challenge is not physical, but one of setting priorities to create time to be active.

**Time Limited** -The time frame is 24 hours.

Ten thousand steps is indeed a very SMART goal.

*It's not good enough for things to be planned – they still have to be done: for the intention to become a reality, energy has to be put into operation.*

Pir Vilayat Inayat Khan

*No farmer every plowed a field by turning it over in his mind.*

Anonymous

## Getting to 10,000

As I noted earlier, there's nothing magic about the number 10,000. However, for most adults in North America it provides an attainable goal, which will mean taking the time to do up to an hour's walking beyond the daily demands of home and work. This is not as difficult as it sounds and this chapter will suggest many ways to "find" enough steps to get you to 10,000.

> Roger Ebert, the film critic, would not describe himself as an athlete, but he is walking, watching his diet and losing weight. In an interview with Ed Lewine of the New York Times (02/13/05) he said, *I usually get up around 7:00 and make my oatmeal. Then I take an hour-long walk: outside if the weather's good; on my treadmill if it's cold. I wear a pedometer, a little device that counts every step. It works as a goad, because you walk additional distances to pile up the numbers. The average person walks 2,000 to 3,000 steps a day. I walk 10,000 steps a day. I have lost a lot of weight as a result.*

When you first get your pedometer it's not a bad idea to wear it for a week without attempting to get any 'extra' steps. This will provide a good picture of your activity lifestyle, and the number of steps you typically average each day.

### Examples of Different Lifestyles and Professions

Note: There can be tremendous variation here. I have provided some typical figures from my own observations and readings.

**Steps Per Day**

| | |
|---|---|
| Person with sedentary job who commutes by car and spends evenings eating and watching TV. | 2500 – 3500 |
| Home based worker who does some chores around the house. | 3000 - 4500 |

*Traveling on foot
can broaden your mind,
while having the opposite effect
on other parts of the anatomy.*

Georgia V. Alan

The British physician, George Cheyne,
wrote a best-selling book, *An Essay of Health
and a Long Life* in 1724. The genesis of the
book was Cheyne's struggle to regain his own
health. He had become enormous and
weighed 445lbs (202kg) before he turned to
diet and exercise. He described many
exercises for his readers but nominated
walking as the best.
*Walking is the most natural and most useful
exercise* was the conclusion of Dr. Cheyne.

## Steps Per Day

| | |
|---|---|
| Stay-at-home mother/father of pre-school children (there's a big variation here depending on whether the children are taken on walks or the parent participates in lots of active play). | 3000 - 8000 |
| A standing job, which involves some movement, though not a lot of specific walking. (e.g. Retail sales clerk, customer service agent at bank or airport). | 5000 - 7500 |
| Active nurses and waitpersons. | Usually get more than 10,000 steps on the job. |
| Walking job, such as letter carrier. We put a pedometer on Mike, the Speakwell mailman (see www.speakwell.com/well/2004spring/pedCopy2.html). Our gardener likewise logs over 20,000 steps a day. | His normal route is nearly 20,000 steps. |

In a piece of US research involving 239 workers including teachers, office clerks, administrators, technical workers, retired people, housewives and people on vacation at home, the average number of steps per day was 4551. Highest of the groups were elementary school teachers, who averaged 6730.

Every job and every person is different, but if you have a sedentary job and commute by car it's unlikely that your daily total will exceed 5,000 steps. Recent research has pointed out the dangers of the suburban lifestyle where communities are designed for cars and not pedestrians. You have to **drive** to the shopping centre, medical building, school and even the fitness club. In contrast, the downtown, urban lifestyle often means **walking** to the store, café, work and other locations because they are nearby, traffic is difficult and parking is either impossible or very expensive. Many urbanites also include a walk to and from subway, bus or train station as part of the rhythm of their days.

*Any idea can be amazing, but it's absolutely useless unless we choose to act on it.*

Simon Ibell

Simon is one of my former students who was born with a disease called Mucopolysaccharidosis (MPS), which meant he'd never reach 5ft (1.5m) tall, would always deal with pain and would probably die well before his 20<sup>th</sup> birthday. Simon ignored the predictions and came to the University of Victoria and, against all odds, obtained his degree in the School of Physical Education. Simon came to work for Speakwell and conceived the idea of a 500k (312mile) bike ride to raise money for, and awareness of, MPS. Every great athlete on Vancouver Island rode with him, including NBA MVP Steve Nash and Olympic Gold Medal winner Simon Whitfield. Simon Ibell was awarded the Spirit of Sport Award on national TV and now works for the global Right to Play movement to raise money for children in underprivileged countries to be involved in sport.

Steve Nash and his friend, Simon Ibell

www.speakwell.com/2004spring

Dana Sullivan picked out representative women in various countries and had them wear a Sportbrain pedometer.

| | **Steps** |
|---|---|
| Mia Petree (suburban) age 33. Arlington, VA, USA (garden work and shopping) | 4,138 |
| Florence Labedays (urban) age 59, Paris, France (Train to and from work, errands, evening out. Does not own a car). | 13,522 |

Once you have familiarized yourself with a typical step-count for your day, select a reasonable target and a strategy for reaching it. **Remember** *every step counts* **so put your pedometer on first thing in the morning, and keep it on until you go to bed.**

Set a reasonable goal and **do everything you can to achieve it.** Steven Covey says that if you want to feel good about yourself, *Make a promise and keep it.* We live in a permissive culture that excuses laziness and poor performance and is afraid of the word "failure". **This easy acceptance of less than our best is one of the primary reasons why we are fatter and less fit than at any time in our history**. The successful steppers I know, and that includes myself, have a non-negotiable agreement with themselves and do everything in their power to achieve their daily goal.

If your stepping target is 8,000 steps, you do not go to bed until your pedometer clicks over to 8,000. Sure ways to destroy your program are thought patterns such as: "I did 12,000 steps yesterday and I'm tired this evening so it's OK if I only do 4,000 today." Learn to value your words. "Every day" means "**every** day" or "6 days a week" means just that: "10,000 steps" means 10,000 steps. One of the saddest situations is if you make a 'promise' to yourself, knowing that you probably won't stick to it. If **you** don't believe in yourself, who else will? Having said that, there will be times

I often smile when people tell me they don't have time to walk. So many great writers, scholars and leaders have made walking an indispensable part of their busy day. People like Charles Dickens, Rousseau, Thoreau and Harry Truman were all dedicated walkers. Thomas Jefferson was a great walker, but also found time to help build a fledgling democracy and work on the Declaration of Independence. In their book *Pedometer Walking*, Mark Fenton and Dave Bassett include an interesting nugget of information about Jefferson's observations regarding a pedometer he bought in France. In summer he averaged 2066 steps per mile, but his *brisk walk of winter* went down to 1735 steps. Presumably in winter he lengthened his stride and picked up the pace to keep himself warm.

when life and circumstances make it unrealistic for you to reach your daily goal. For instance, you or one of your children is sick; you have to deal with an emergency situation or you sustain an injury. If this happens, it's not a reason to abandon the program, it's just the reality of life getting in the way and you do the best you can in the circumstances. Then go right back to your chosen program as soon as possible. It's important that you feel in control and that you don't miss your steps for trivial reasons. Excuses such as, *We've got people coming to dinner, I'm a bit tired, It's raining, I can't miss the Oscars* are not acceptable if you want to make a real difference to your life.

### The Major Walk

Part of every stepping program should contain one purposeful walk of half an hour **at the very least.**
**Note**: Some of the better pedometers record the uninterrupted steps of a sustained walk as "aerobic steps", so that at the end of the day you can separate your intermittent house and work based steps from continuous walking steps.

On your major daily walk you are getting much more than steps.

(I) You get an excellent cardiovascular stimulus. When walking, it's like having 3 hearts, one in your chest and one in each leg squeezing the blood around with every step.

(II) You get time to think. Many writers use walking to unblock their thoughts and free-up their creative processes. Charles Dickens, walked up to 20 miles some days, and created many of the great characters in his novels while in motion. Nietzsche noted that, *All truly great thoughts are conceived by walking.*

(III) Sustained walking is a form of meditation. **In the repetitive movement of walking you can find stillness.** Angels whisper louder when you walk and as Matthew Henry noted, "It is not talking, but walking that will bring us to heaven."

(IV) Stress is relieved by walking. Earlier, I noted the old Latin proverb, "Solvitur Ambulando" (It is solved by walking). For more information on the control of stress by walking see Chapter 7, 'Walking and Stress'.

(V) Even if you are getting a lot of incidental steps at work or by playing with your children, the major walk should still be part of

*By getting their owners out walking on a regular basis, dogs really are a man's (or a woman's) best friend. It's not just Lassie that saves lives, but every pooch who shames their owner into getting up from the couch and going for a life-saving, health enhancing walk.*

Martin Collis

your day. Continuous walking has a rhythm that is different from the discontinuous steps of work or play. There is a different pace, a time to clear your mind and a few minutes to separate yourself from the demands of the day.

### When is the best time to walk?

The easy answer to the above question is, whenever you can find time in your day. This, of course is true, but not particularly helpful. The best time to walk is early in the morning; it is a great way to start your day. People who are most successful at sticking to an exercise program are the early birds. If you get up and get out before most people are awake, the phones won't ring, only sadists hold meetings, and nobody wants a piece of your time. If you are really lucky you might be able to walk to work and arrive awake and refreshed while your colleagues are hitting the coffee machine hoping in vain for the same feeling. Psychologically, it is satisfying to have been up and moving before the day has really begun, to start the business of the day with 5 or 6 thousand steps already under your belt.

An interesting study at the Fred Hutchinson Cancer Research Center in Seattle discovered early morning aerobic exercisers were about 70% less likely to have trouble sleeping than other early risers who exercised less or not at all. Lead researcher Anne McTiernan theorizes that morning walking may help adjust the internal clock that governs the sleep/wake cycle. While in contrast, evening exercise may hinder sleep by temporarily boosting metabolism and triggering the release of nerve-stimulating hormones. McTiernan added that stretching and muscle relaxation at any time seems to promote restful sleep.

Having said that early morning walking is best; I know it is not for everybody. It is not practical for some and just not right for others who have no desire to win the mind over mattress battle. There is a long tradition of lunchtime exercise for people taking a break from work. A lunchtime walk or workout breaks up the day and can send you back to work in the afternoon refreshed and reinvigorated. A colleague said that

*Walk a hound, lose a pound.*

Motto of a dog-walking
group in Lubbock, Texas

*Walk your dog everyday, whether or not you
have a dog.*

Paul Dudley White

his lunch hour walk gave him a *two morning day*. Steps are just as valuable in the evening, but harder to come by. You are often tired and want to sit down to dinner, to play with your children or watch the evening news. The most successful evening walkers are dog owners who might deprive themselves of exercise, but cannot say *no* to their dog.

### You Must Have a Plan

*You plan to fail by failing to plan.*
John L. Beckley

The important thing is to plan your walking time and schedule it into your day. If you tell yourself you'll take a walk when you have some time later, it won't happen. It's like saying you'll save money if you have some left over at the end of the month. The rule is to **pay yourself first.** Set aside time for your walk before it gets crowded out by other events. Many, many walking and exercise programs die a logistical death. Walking will save your life, and what meeting, chore, TV show or conversation could be more important than that?

At the University of Victoria I was a member of the slowest jogging group on campus, known as the 'Escargots'. Our slogan was *No Pain, No Pain*. However, we were dedicated and every lunchtime the Escargots would shuffle around the 5k-chip trail. If people asked me to attend a lunchtime meeting I'd politely tell them that I had another commitment. I'd return to my office in the afternoon showered, renewed and ready to take on the challenges of the 2nd half of the day.

### Social or Solitary Walking

The old song says that, *You'll never walk alone* , but in pursuit of your 10,000 steps there are times when you will have to, with only your thoughts for company. Having a partner or group can add a pleasant social dimension to your steps and you'll find that walking and talking go well together. At times you can combine walking and business. As a professor

*If not now, when?*

Hebrew saying

*Who are mighty? They who conquer themselves.*

Hebrew saying from
*Ethics of our Fathers*

I'd often talk through a problem with a graduate student while walking round campus and many business professionals have discovered the effectiveness of a walking meeting. Counselors and psychologists have also found that selected sessions go better when walking with a client rather than sitting with them.

Some walkers use an iPod or Discman to provide a sound track to their steps, others listen to a radio or chat on a cell phone, it doesn't matter just as long as walking is part of your day.

So take your pick, early morning, lunchtime, late afternoons, evening; with dog or dogless; on your own, on the phone or with a friend, every step is a step in the right direction.

### Practical Ways of Adding Steps to Your Days

Walk around while talking on your cell phone or cordless phone.
Walk around the field or rink if your child is playing or practicing.
Use stairs whenever possible.
Use some planned inefficiency:
Take some extra trips with your grocery bags.
Walk to a co-worker's office rather than send an email.
Walk to the mailbox.
Always return your grocery cart.
Deliver fliers.
Walk to the local store regularly rather than doing a huge shop at a supermarket.
Use a bathroom on another floor or different part of the house or workplace.
Walk at airports while waiting for a flight. (A big source of steps for me.)
Walk your dog.
Volunteer for anything involving walking:
Rake or mow the lawn of an elderly or infirm neighbor.
Walk a friend's dog while they're away.
Do some walking errands for housebound neighbors.
At work, always be ready to deliver a package or any other task that requires walking.
Get a treadmill so you can walk at home whatever the weather.
Walk to the movies.

# There's 10,000 Ways to Lose Your Blubber

### (with apologies to Paul Simon)

*Just get off the bus, Gus*
*Put on some new shoes, Suze,*
*Pick up the pace, Ace,*
*Your body's a disgrace.*
*There's 10,000 ways to lose your blubber.*

*Go on a hike, Mike,*
*Cut out the carbs, Barb,*
*10,000 a day, Ray,*
*You know what I say.*
*There's 10,000 ways to lose your blubber.*

Walk with your children.
Walk around the shopping mall.
Walk during TV commercials.
Walk while listening to a talking book or to music.
Get off the bus or train one or two stops early and walk the rest of the way.
Park a short walk away from your office.
Walk in your garden or nearby park and follow the seasonal changes.
Walk around your house or apartment and make one improvement, such as picking up, tidying or rearranging.
Walk your children to school.

---

### Snacking

Many diets are destroyed by snacking, when calories are consumed almost unnoticed in between meals and throughout the evening. *Active Snacking* turns this concept around. Instead of taking in extra calories by snacking on food, you burn off a few extra calories by *snacking* on exercise. An active snack might be a walk to the mailbox or corner store, it could be a walk around your garden or a local park, or it might just be walking on the spot during TV commercials. The old song says, *Little Things Mean a Lot,* and they do in love, life and step counting

---

It's been estimated that the use of a TV remote control instead of getting up and manually changing channels accounts for more than 1 lb of weight gained per year for the average TV watcher. The original remote was called a *Lazybones* and was manufactured by Zenith. How can we not gain weight if we sit in our *La-Z-Boy* chair, with built in beer holder and aim our *Lazybones* remote at the TV? You can't say the manufacturers didn't warn you with their descriptive names.

Initially, you might have to be a bit obsessive to keep coming up with 10,000 steps each day, but within a few weeks it becomes easy and natural,

*I am not one of those people who claims she loves to exercise. I simply love all that it does for me.*

Oprah Winfrey

*A person's health can be judged by which he takes two at a time – pills or stairs.*

Joan Welsh

and the pay off in feeling good is self-evident. In the past week I'll give you 3 examples of 'finding' some extra steps. I live on Vancouver Island and sometimes have to use a ferry. The ferry was late and during the 1-hour wait while most people sat in their cars or made a pilgrimage to the food services, I walked 5000 steps and figured out some ideas for my newsletter. Two days later I was at the local hospital where I was having a cast removed from my wrist. I was given a number and found there were 23 people ahead of me. Instead of taking my place in the corridor on the hospital chairs, which are designed for stacking rather than comfort, and complaining about the health care service understaffing, I walked the hospital corridors and grounds. I went past one of the saddest tableaux just outside the doors of the hospital where the smokers congregate with their IV drips, wheelchairs, hacking coughs and despair. Lastly, I found a stepping device at a garage sale and now crank up the TV or stereo and get some hardworking steps in my own den.

**If it's steps you want, they're there for the taking, but you might have to rearrange your thinking to see extra walking as a bonus rather than a problem to be avoided at all costs.**

### 10,000 and Beyond

*Form good habits, they're just as hard to break as bad ones.*

How you approach becoming a 10,000 step a day person might depend on your fitness, your job or your personality. There's a lot to be said for the Nike slogan of *Just Do It*, For many people, adding 4 or 5 thousand steps to their day in order to reach 10,000 is not a physical challenge, but an organizational challenge. By walking early and walking often it's surprising how quickly your pedometer will be registering 10,000.

A reminder here: **Record Your Steps**!! One of the biggest benefits of using a pedometer is that it makes you deal with reality. Without a specific goal and without a way to measure and record your steps it's so easy to kid yourself that you're doing enough. You can keep a logbook, or better still, go to Speakwell.com and record your steps on PED. I'll repeat the words of Tom Peters, *What gets measured gets done*.

*Success is not something you wait for, but something you work for.*

Henry W. Longfellow

If you've not been used to walking much at all, or have some physical restrictions, or maybe like to approach things gradually, then begin by recording your average daily steps for a typical week and try increasing that number by 1000 steps per day for the following week. If you are able to achieve this for a week or two, add another 1000. Weight lifters call this 'progressive resistance training', which is increasing the resistance (in your case the number of steps) until a desired goal is reached, or even exceeded.

The strategy you use is up to you and anything is fine as long as it results in you making a significant increase to your walking. Remember that W.E.L.L.* is an acronym for Walk Everyday, Live Longer (not to mention live better). *Acronym from Guy le Mesurier

Personally, I like to get at least 10,000 steps every day. I wear one of Lance Armstrong's *LiveStrong* yellow bands on my wrist as a reminder and a reward for getting to 10,000. If I miss a day, I have to remove the elastic bracelet and have to 'earn' it back, by doing 7 consecutive days in which I get to 15,000 steps or more. It might sound obsessive but you don't change your life by being half hearted or average.

In 2005 I only missed my 10,000-step target once and that was by choice in order not to disrupt a family gathering. At times it was a challenge. I recently played most of the day in a bridge tournament and then went out to dinner and at 9:30 in the evening still needed 4000 steps. While other people went to the lounge bar, I put on my hat, scarf and coat and set out around the city streets to get my steps. It wasn't a *fun* walk, I didn't have any great thoughts and I regretted not having done a longer walk in the morning but 40 minutes later I felt a certain satisfaction that I'd earned the right to wear my *LiveStrong* band and quietly sang the old Beatles song *You know it don't come easy*.

The inspirational quotation below is often attributed to Goethe in its entirety. In fact, it was written by W. H. Murray in a 1951 book *The Scottish Himalayan Expedition*. Murray closed his message with a couplet loosely translated from Goethe's *Faust*.

*Until one is committed*
*There is hesitancy, the chance to draw back,*
*Always ineffectiveness.*
*Concerning all acts of initiative (and creation),*
*There is one elementary truth,*
*The ignorance of which kills countless ideas*
*And splendid plans:*
*That the moment one definitely commits oneself,*
*Then Providence moves too.*
*All sorts of things occur to help one*
*That would never otherwise have occurred.*
*A whole stream of events issues from the decision*
*Raising in one's favor all manner*
*Of unforeseen incidents and meetings*
*And material assistance,*
*Which no man could have dreamt*
*Would have come his way.*

William Hutchinson Murray

*Whatever you can do, or dream you can, begin it.*
*Boldness has genius, power, and magic in it.*

Goethe

### Your First Million

| 10,000 | 10,000 | | | | | | | | |
|--------|--------|---|---|---|---|---|---|---|---|
| | | | | | | | | | |
| | | | | | | | | | |
| | | | | | | | | | |
| | | | | | | | | | |
| | | | | | | | | | |
| | | | | | | | | | |
| | | | | | | | | | |
| | | | | | | | | | |
| | | | | | | | | | |

Each rectangle represents 10,000 steps, just keep crossing them off until you've completed the large rectangle and have successfully achieved your first million. For a person of average weight a million steps represent about 15lbs lost, or at least 15lbs not gained.

REWARD: (write your own reward)_____

If you like something a bit more colorful and stimulating than just crossing off little boxes, you can purchase the *One Million Footstep Challenge* from Creative Walking Inc., PO Box 50296, Clayton, MO 63105 USA. They offer sheets of heart-shaped stickers, which you can put in your logbook or on a wall chart.

Get a good pedometer, set a S.M.A.R.T. goal and remember the words of William Murray and Goethe shown on the facing page.

*If you don't design your own life plan,
chances are you'll fall into someone else's plan.
Guess what they have planned for you?
Not much!!*

Jim Rohn

*Keep not standing fixed and rooted
Briskly venture, briskly roam.*

Goethe

## Pick a Practical Pedometer

**Note:** In the words of the Talking Heads there might be *too much information* in this section for some readers, but there is such variation among pedometers that I felt it was important to provide you with a method to assess the quality of your pedometer and do some consumer research on your behalf. If you just wish to see my top recommendation in each of 3 different price ranges, turn to the end of the chapter.

In many ways pedometers are like wristwatches. The primary function of a watch is to reliably tell you the correct time. If your watch can't be relied on to reflect the correct time, it doesn't matter what it looks like, whether it gives you phases of the moon, has an alarm feature and other functions, it's a useless watch. The same applies to pedometers, their primary role is to count and record your steps and if they don't do that, all the other design features and extras are irrelevant.

In assessing pedometers I've divided them into two categories, namely: (i) Step-only pedometers, which record your step count and nothing more and (ii) Multi-function pedometers, which provide additional information, such as estimated distance walked and calories burned.

Pedometry is not a precise science, during the course of a day we will do all manner of half steps, shuffle steps, balancing steps and incidental moves that may or may not be recorded and **it doesn't matter**. We are not doing research in which we need to record every micro-movement; we are looking for a practical recording device, which reflects our general activity level. The word pedometer has its roots in the Latin word 'ped', which means foot, and as the word suggests it means things we do on foot and not activities such as swimming, weight training, Pilates or yoga. Although pedometers are not designed to be used while cycling, I choose to leave mine on my belt when I ride and have noticed that it does record some 'steps'. This is something you might wish to try for yourself, or you may choose to keep your pedometer exclusively for walking, jogging or other step related activities. I have found that a pedometer keeps a good count of my rotations on an elliptical trainer and can also be used on a home 'stepper' and, of course, in the increasingly popular pole walking.

*Don't substitute frenzied activity for the joy of routine physical activity.*

Peter C. Whybrow

### How to Wear Your Pedometer

This is very important; the pedometer should be worn as close as possible to the top point of the hipbone. It will clip onto a belt or an elastic waistband (Note: When clipped onto an elastic waistband there is a tendency for a pedometer to 'jump' off when the pants are taken down, e.g. when going to the bathroom. This problem can be solved by attaching a very inexpensive 'leash' to the pedometer, which provides a secondary safety clip.) I discovered the importance of correct pedometer placement in an experimental series in which I compared results of placing pedometers on the point of the hip with ones in which the pedometer was worn closer to the center of the body (Approximately half way between the hip and navel, more or less above the knee.) The more central placement produced results that were so inaccurate and unreliable that after 20 tests there was no point in continuing the series. Most manufacturers do a good job in describing the optimal placement of a pedometer, however, the instructions accompanying a Kellogg's promotional pedometer were not only misleading but also good for a smile. This was obviously a less than perfect translation into English.

> *The paces are detected via the movement of waist.* [Glad they spelled that correctly]
> *Attach the step counter securely to your waistband or belt, close to the center of your body.* [Wrong]
> *False mounting will possibly arouse inaccurate result.* [It was ever thus]

For people who have either aesthetic or practical reasons why they can't wear a pedometer on a waistband or belt, the Omron HJ112 can be worn in a small pouch around the neck or carried in a pocket.

### How Pedometers Work

You don't need to know how your pedometer works in order to use it successfully any more than you need to understand your car's engine in order to drive. Suffice to say there are a few different mechanisms, which enable pedometers to count your steps. The most common is the (i) hairspring pedometer, which is generally considered to be somewhat less

*Let no one be deluded that a knowledge
of the path can substitute for putting
one foot in front of the other.*

Mary Catherine Richards

reliable and long lasting than the more expensive (ii) coil spring pedometer. Another type of mechanism is the (iii) magnetic reed proximity switch (MRPS), which seems to be quite dependent on its design and the quality of its manufacturing. I note this because some makes, which use this technology, are accurate and dependable, whereas others are much less so. Finally, there is (iv) the accelerometer type of mechanism, which tends to be the most sensitive and expensive and is excellent for research or for someone who needs precise information about caloric expenditure.

### Picking a Good Pedometer

How do you pick a good pedometer? I feel this is a question I can answer as well as anybody. Because of my work with Circle Canada and Route 66 and with various group walking projects, I've talked with hundreds of people about the reliability, effectiveness and pricing of a variety of pedometers. When I decided to market pedometers my due diligence led me to devise a 25-point scale for multi-function pedometers and a 20-point scale for step-only pedometers. I tried to look at pedometers from the point of view of ordinary consumers, not from that of university based researchers. I assembled 25 popular makes and models of pedometers for evaluation.

### The Perfect, Practical, Multi-Function Pedometer

The perfect, practical multi-function pedometer would get its 25 points as follows:

| | |
|---|---|
| Within 1% accuracy on repeated trials at 2mph walking | 5 points |
| Within 1% accuracy on repeated trials at 4mph walking | 5 points |
| Price below $25 CDN or $20 USD (Providing the Pedometer is within 6% accuracy) | 3 points |
| Strong spring clip (Important so pedometers don't get lost) | 1 point |
| Cover (so the buttons don't get accidentally re-set) | 1 point |
| Easy-to-read display | 1 point |
| Easy-to-use buttons | 1 point |
| 7-day memory of daily step counts | 1 point |
| Calories burned | 1 point |
| Distance covered | 1 point |
| Clock | 1 point |
| Supporting print information (good instructions) | 1 point |

*Our greatest glory is not in always succeeding,*
*but in rising up every time we fail.*

Ralph Waldo Emerson

*I get knocked down, but I get up again.*

Chumbawumba

| | |
|---|---|
| Other useful features | up to 3 points |
| (e.g. Backlighting, timer, separate aerobic steps, radio, sensitivity adjustment etc.) | |
| **Total** | **25 points** |

The study we conducted at Speakwell was not definitive research, it was a careful look at a variety of pedometers, which had been purchased from local stores, from web sites, sent to us by manufacturers or distributors and even obtained 'free' from McDonalds and Kellogg's. We looked at form (design) and function (performance). Our hope was to provide consumers with a practical way to evaluate pedometers.

The most significant part of the testing was accuracy of step counting. In order to assess this, each pedometer was monitored on 8 separate 200-step walks on a treadmill; 4 at 2mph (3.2km) and 4 at 4mph (6.4km). If 7 consistent scores were obtained and one was out of place, we ran one retest in case there had been some flaw in the testing procedure, such as pedometer placement. Many pedometers functioned well at 4mph, which is faster than most people walk, but were less reliable at 2mph, which is a lot closer to the typical walking speed of people throughout the day. In calculating the accuracy of a pedometer we quickly discovered that it was no use just averaging the totals of the 8 200-step walks. For instance, if a pedometer recorded 250 steps for one 200-step walk and 150 steps for the next, the average would be 200 (250 + 150 = 400/2 = 200), which looks perfect, when in fact it miscounted by 50 steps on each walk. Therefore, we had to look at how much the step count differed from 200; whether it was over counting or undercounting. Using the previous example, the step count would be 50 steps over 200 and 50 steps under 200 for a total of 100 miscounted steps in two walks. Expressed as a percentage this would show 25% error in recorded steps (100 miscounted steps out of 400 steps walked).

### Rating Pedometer Step Recording Accuracy on a 5-Point Scale

Any pedometer that was within 3% accuracy at both speeds is acceptable for day-to-day step counting (n.b. Pedometers manufactured and marketed in Japan are required to be within 3% accuracy by law). In putting a numerical value to pedometers we awarded points for accuracy as follows:

An often overlooked study, which reinforces the importance of step-count in weight control.

### Physical Activity and Human Obesity

A.M. Chirico and A.J. Stunkard
New England Journal of Medicine 263:935-940, 1960

The study looked at the distance walked, as measured by a pedometer, of a large group of obese and non-obese men and women working in a variety of different jobs.

The average distance walked by the obese women was about 2.9 miles (4.6km) less than that walked by the non-obese women. Total miles walked each day averaged 2.0 miles (4000 steps) for the obese and 4.9 miles (just about 10,000 steps) for the non-obese. The data for the men showed a similar pattern. The obese men averaged 3.5 miles a day (7000 steps) while their non-obese counterparts averaged 5.8 miles a day (10,800 steps).
(I should note that this average figure for the men was boosted by mileage totals by a stockroom clerk, laborer and medical student.)

### Percentage Error

| Points | 2mph | 4mph |
|:------:|:----:|:----:|
| 5 | 1% | 1% |
| 4 | 2% | 2% |
| 3 | 3% | 3% |
| 2 | 4% | 4% |
| 1 | 5% | 5% |

A pedometer that was within 1% of the actual step-count over 4 trials at the fast speed or 4 trials at the slow speed was awarded 5 points, so that a really accurate pedometer would score a total of 10 points.

### Example:

My Health XL15 Pedometer
Actual steps recorded for 4 200-step trials at 4mph (6.4km):

| | | | |
|---|---|---|---|
| 200 | 199 | 202 | 200 |

So at 4mph the XL15 was only 3 steps away from perfect, giving it a percentage error of 0.375%, which is well under 1%, for a 5 point score at 4mph.

Actual steps recorded for 4 200-step trials at 2mph (3.2km):

| | | | |
|---|---|---|---|
| 201 | 197 | 208 | 202 |

At the slower speed there was a slight decrease in the accuracy of recording, with 14 mis-recorded steps. In this case the percentage error is 1.75%, which is less than 2%, giving it a score of 4 points at 2mph.

### Pedometers

If you don't own a pedometer why not consider buying one? You'll get more out of this book, more out of your walks and maybe more out of life. They can be little lifechangers.

If you do own a pedometer take it out for a test walk. Walk quickly for 200 steps and check your pedometer step total, then stroll for 200 steps. A good pedometer will be very close to 200 for both the fast and slow walks. A less reliable pedometer will miss a number of steps when you walk slowly.

## Table 1      Percentage of Error for All 25 Pedometers Tested

| Pedometer -make and model | Accuracy at 2mph (3.2km) Points out of 5 | % of error | Accuracy at 4mph (6.4km) Points out of 5 | % of error | Within 5% accuracy at both speeds. |
|---|---|---|---|---|---|
| Multi-function Models | | | | | |
| Blue Cross/Blue Shield | 0 | 51.5 | 0 | 20 | No |
| Freestyle 599 Coach | 0 | 6 | 5 | 0.75 | No |
| Freestyle Ergo Touch 591 | 1 | 4.625 | 5 | 0.625 | Yes |
| Freestyle Tracer | 0 | 11.75 | 3 | 2.375 | No |
| LifeGear | 3 | 2.125 | 4 | 1.375 | Yes |
| My Health X08 | 0 | 8.875 | 2 | 3.25 | No |
| My Health XL15 | 4 | 1.75 | 5 | 0.375 | Yes |
| New-Lifestyles NL2000 | 4 | 2 | 5 | 1 | Yes |
| New-Lifestyles SW700 | 3 | 2.125 | 5 | 0.625 | Yes |
| Omron HJ-105 | 4 | 1.625 | 5 | 0.375 | Yes |
| Omron HJ-112 | 5 | 0.625 | 5 | 0.25 | Yes |
| Oregon Scientific Pe316FM | 1 | 4.5 | 2 | 3.25 | Yes |
| Oregon Scientific Pe316CA | 0 | 13.375 | 3 | 2.375 | No |
| SAHO Step It UP Digital Ez-V | 5 | 0.5 | 4 | 1.125 | Yes |
| Speakwell H215 | 4 | 1.375 | 5 | 0.5 | Yes |
| StMoritz Digiwalker SW500 | 0 | 7.25 | 5 | 0.875 | Yes |
| Step-only Models | | | | | |
| 10 K a Day | 0 | 9.375 | 3 | 2.625 | No |
| Accusplit | 0 | 30.125 | 4 | 2 | No |
| Active Living Alliance | 4 | 1.375 | 4 | 1.25 | Yes |
| Kellogg's Pedometer Giveaway | 0 | 15.5 | 2 | 4 | No |
| McDonalds Go Active | 0 | 42.75 | 0 | 11.875 | No |
| New Lifestyles Digiwalker SW-200 | 3 | 2.75 | 5 | 0.125 | Yes |
| Omron HJ-002 | 2 | 3.375 | 4 | 2 | Yes |
| Step Diet Accusplit Eagle 1020 | 0 | 27.375 | 4 | 1.25 | No |
| Small Steps/Big Rewards HM FP002 | 0 | 17.625 | 2 | 3.125 | No |

*On a recent trip to New York I found a
matchbook from the 1950s featuring a pedometer.
I don't know how accurate it was, or what
mechanism it used, but the price of $3.99 seemed
reasonable.*

## Top Pedometers for Step Counting Accuracy

Price is not a consideration in these ratings. It will be a factor in Table 3.

### Table 2

| Pedometer make and model | Points for accuracy out of 10 |
|---|:---:|
| **Multi-function models** | |
| Omron HJ112 | 10 |
| Digital EZ-V (SAHO Step-it-up) | 9 |
| Speakwell H215 | 9 |
| New Lifestyles NL2000 | 9 |
| Omron HJ105 | 9 |
| My Health XL15 | 9 |
| New Lifestyle Digi-Walker SW700 | 8 |
| Life Gear | 7 |
| Freestyle Ergo-Touch 591 | 6 |
| **Step-Only Models** | |
| Active Living Alliance** | 8 |
| New Lifestyle Digi-Walker SW200 | 8 |

**Active Living Alliance pedometer is included as part of the Stepping Out program in some Canadian provinces.

Before showing our overall findings, I will reiterate that this is not the definitive rating of pedometers; in fact no such list exists. There are hundreds of pedometers out there and we have neither the time or budget to assess them all. We would like to have tested multiples of each model selected, but again time and budget constraints did not permit this. What this will provide you with is a template for assessing any pedometer in which you are interested. It will also give you our findings, testing 25 pedometers using male and female subjects on each test on 8 standardized 200-step treadmill walks. A few of our ratings, such as quality of display, type of clip and ease of use of buttons, are subjective. There is a great variability in price and our estimates were based on averaging an Internet search.

Appropriately, by far the heaviest weight is given to accuracy. The next

*Now shall I walk, or shall I ride?*
*"Ride" pleasure said, "Walk" joy replied.*

W. H. Davis

heaviest weighting is given for price, because in supplying pedometers to schools, hospitals, seniors' centers and various employee groups we have found cost to be a very significant consideration. However, it is pointless to save money by purchasing unreliable pedometers. If people record their steps, the 7-day memory feature is extremely useful and personally I enjoy using a pedometer that has the capability to 'store' my steps.

To see the detailed tables of results go to www.speakwell.com/well/2005autumn/pedometer.php. Scroll down to see Master Table 3 (page 1 and 2) and click on the link.

### Observations

(I)   Pedometers are nearly always more accurate recording fast walking than slow walking. The only pedometer that tested slightly more accurate at a slow speed was the Ez-V (SAHO).

(II)  We were somewhat surprised that the Digiwalker line (although good) did lose some accuracy at the slower walking speed. Our surprise came from the fact that some researchers have described Digiwalkers as the 'gold standard' for pedometry. A few researchers have actually evaluated other pedometers by comparing them with a Digiwalker. With their premium pricing and lack of extras the three Digiwalkers we tested did not score as highly as I would have anticipated.

(III) A surprisingly effective pedometer was a customized model distributed by My Health and SAHO. Because of different packaging and branding we did not realize they were in fact identical models until closer inspection after the treadmill testing. They are relatively inexpensive, have an excellent display and each independently scored a 9 out of 10 points for accuracy.

**Note:** We were sufficiently impressed with the price and performance of the SAHO and My Health pedometers that we contacted the manufacturer and have imported the identical model to be distributed by Speakwell (SPEAKWELL H215).

*After dinner rest awhile,*
*After supper walk a mile.*

Arabic proverb

*It is exercise alone that supports the spirits, and*
*keeps the mind in vigor.*

Cicero

## Best Buys

**High End** (Typically priced over $35 Canadian or $29 US)

**Best Buy**: Omron HJ-112

The Japanese based Omron Healthcare Inc. markets a variety of medical instruments including a line of pedometers. The HJ-112 with its accelerator sensors was the only pedometer we tested to score a perfect 10 points for accuracy. In our overall scoring the only points it lost were for pricing, as it is a sophisticated piece of equipment. If worn on your belt in the traditional way it slides into a holster to hold it in place, but it also tested out extremely well when carried in a small pocket, in a bag or around the neck. A noise reduction algorithm excludes incidental movement such as standing up/sitting down, car driving and other micro-movements. As noted earlier, the effectiveness of the HJ-112 was reported at the October 2005 ACSM Walking for Health Conference in papers by Hassen et al. And Roberts et al.

For research work, or if I simply wanted an excellent pedometer I would select the Omron HJ-112 over the comparably priced New Lifestyles NL2000 and the Digiwalker SW700, because of its accuracy, its flexibility of placement and its features.

Our findings were in line with Consumer Reports October 2004 issue, who only rated one pedometer, the Omron HJ-112, in their "Excellent" category. They, too, placed it ahead of the New Lifestyles 2000, which was rated "Very Good" and the Digiwalkers SW700 and SW701, which were rated only "Good" (see 'Well' Fall 2004).

*Note: In the United States, WalMart have been offering the HJ-112 for $20, which is a fantastic deal.

**Mid-Range Priced Pedometers** (Between $21 - $35 Canadian, or about $17 - $29 US)

**Best Buy**: Omron HJ-105

The Omron HJ-105 had the highest total points score and would be my selection for a multi-function pedometer in the mid-price range. It scored

*The key to the human potential movement
is movement.*

Unknown

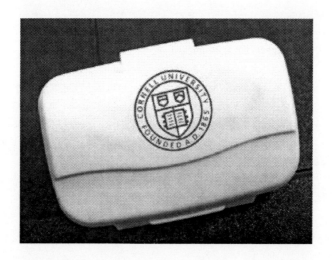

Speakwell H215 pedometer customized for Cornell University

9 out of 10 points for accuracy, 2 for pricing and comes with a variety of useful features including a 7-day memory and an ability to separate continuous aerobic steps from intermittent steps. It has a variable sensitivity lever, which some critics regard as a deficit, but which I have found very functional. Some older people and obese people don't have a lot of leg lift when they walk and often need enhanced sensitivity on their pedometers in order to more accurately reflect their step count. It is interesting that in other evaluations I have seen, no one has adjusted the sensitivity lever for testing.

Speakwell has sold over 10,000 HJ-105s and have had less than 1% returned, indicating good reliability. In one report I read, *Anatomy of a Pedometer* by JSC Engineering, the battery life of the HJ-105 was rated as 'very short'. This has not been my experience; the battery is protected from activation, until after it's unpacked, by a thin plastic strip. I have used the same Omron HJ-105 for my Circle Canada virtual walk and at the time of writing have logged over 6 million steps and I'm on my 3<sup>rd</sup> battery, which is good enough for me.

**Inexpensive Pedometers** (Under $20 Canadian, $17 US)

**Best Buy**: Speakwell H215, My Health XL15 and SAHO Ez-V (same pedometer, different name)

Based on our testing, I would select the above pedometer as my choice in the inexpensive range. It was more accurate than any of the step-only pedometers tested and offered more features. The magnets are not rubber coated so there is a quiet clicking, but it in not intrusive. The H215, XL15 and the Ez-V scored 9 out of 10 for accuracy, rating them the real surprise of the group. They are excellent for any large group and we are carrying them at Speakwell at a generous reduction for bulk purchases. For orders over 1000 units we can customize this pedometer with the company or institutional logo as we did recently for Cornell University. See WellMart for pricing and information regarding class sets for schools. [http://www.speakwell.com/wellMart/index.shtml]

*Everywhere is within walking distance, if you have the time.*

Steven Wright

*So often times it happens*
*We live our lives in chains*
*And never even know*
*We have the key.*

Jack Tempchin and Rob Strandlund

From the *Eagles'* song *Already Gone*

## Closing Comments

This survey has looked at a cross-section of currently available, widely used pedometers. The popularity of pedometry seems to continue to grow and we are already beginning to see the direction in which the next generation of pedometers will evolve. The Omron 700 series is now available in Japan and have the capability of being downloaded into your computer. A number of other companies are in the process of launching downloadable pedometers and I will continue to monitor their evolution.

Even without looking at eBay, one can currently find pedometers, which are built into cell phones and are combined with MP3 players. Others are in shoe insoles, ballpoint pens and can be worn as armbands. Despite the gadgetry and packaging the bottom line remains: does the pedometer accurately count and record your steps? If the price seems too good to be true, it probably is. Caveat emptor still pertains.

*10,000 steps a day will improve your life expectancy. You start expecting more from your life.*

Martin Collis

*Even if you don't live a day longer, you will live a longer day.*

George Sheehan

# 5

# Virtual Walking

## Circle Canada and Route 66

Our ever-increasing access to computers has created a whole different way to translate cumulative steps into an actual, visible journey. A well-constructed virtual journey gives substance to the numbers on your pedometer and translates them into cities and scenery.

I looked at the pedometer-based programs on the web and, in general, found them uninspired and somewhat boring. Following the old maxim that, *if you want something done right, do it yourself* I challenged myself and my computer team of Ron Nye and Luke Niedjalski to come up with a program that would provide visual feedback and on-going interest to people recording their steps. The result was Circle Canada, which we offer at no cost to any individual or group who wish to use it at www.speakwell.com.

In Circle Canada, and now Route 66, as your steps (individual or group) accumulate, a red line will start snaking its way around the country. At each marked city along the way there are pop-ups featuring history, regional festivals, activity and recreation opportunities, famous residents, good places to eat, local humor and points of interest. To help you on your journey, there are occasional *free rides* (it's like Snakes and Ladders with

Once Circle Canada was online my assistant Bev and I set out to complete the 18,000-kilometer circuit of this huge country. It took the two of us nearly two years, with each of us averaging about 12,000 steps a day, to complete the journey.

Our total step count was 16,310,561. This means that we burned about 815,528 calories, which is the equivalent of burning 233lbs of weight (105kg). This is the beauty of walking on a daily basis, at first it might seem insignificant, until it's recorded and totaled to show the life-enhancing value of getting those 10,000 plus steps a day.

By the end of the trip my assistant, Bev, was 40lbs (18kg) lighter while I shed a mere 5lbs (2.2lbs). I guess caloric intake really does make a difference no snakes). On the Prairies, a CN train will suddenly whisk you from Vegreville to Saskatoon, and as you progress you will be delighted to be given a lift on a paddle steamer, hot air ballon, float plane, dog sled team or a Blue Nose Schooner. All of which keeps Circle Canada entertaining and rewarding.

If you want to have a quick journey around the country, just increase the size of the team. A class of school children in the Yukon circled the whole 18,000k (11,000 miles) around the country in 12 weeks and learned a lot of geography, history and social studies that term. Another alternative is to shorten the route and stop at a designated city.

The new Route 66 is shorter than Circle Canada, remember the song which tells us, *It winds from Chicago to LA, more than two thousand miles all the way*. There's a lot of interest and a lot of history along this route, which has been written about and sung about since its inception. Now you can walk it and *get your kicks on Route 66*.

Over the past two years I've recorded some of the comments people have made about Circle Canada. I believe similar sentiments will soon be expressed about our Route 66.

- *Circle Canada is a life changer and difference maker.*
- *Circle Canada is the missing link between pedometer based walking programs and sustained success.*
- *Circle Canada enables you to be a part of a group without actually walking with them.*

To those I add some of my own observations.
- Circle Canada enables you to separate out your individual statistics and see how the miles and kilometers represent weight lost or weight maintained.
- Circle Canada can be used in schools to motivate children to be active and to teach them geography, history and social studies. They are much more interested in an area they have 'walked' to rather than one which is a random dot on a map.
- Circle Canada has the best ROI (Return On Investment), as part of an employee fitness/wellness program, of any that I know, for

Steve Vaught was a 400lb depressed, ex-marine who decided to address his depression and obesity by attempting to walk from sea to shining sea, from the California coast to New York. He became famous as 'Fat Man Walking' and his website **www.thefatmanwalking.com** drew millions of hits. The primary purpose of the journey was one of self-discovery, but by the time he reached New York after his 13-month odyssey, the Fat Man that was walking wasn't quite as fat, he'd lost over 100lbs.

*Circle Canada: I love the whole concept – have been using my pedometer for a couple of months and really enjoying tracking my progress (daily and across Canada). Thanks so much for all the work you have put into this. It's so nice to have something worthwhile to work on and to encourage my kids to work on.*

Jan Thomas

Telus Business Solutions

the following reasons:

(I)    Every employee, whatever their location, with access to a computer, can participate in Circle Canada.

(II)    There is no capital outlay to set up the program. There is no cost for using Circle Canada.

(III)    Walking is the most popular form of physical activity in North America and nearly all employees can walk on a daily basis.

(IV)    People with disabilities who use a wheel chair can record distance traveled and convert it into steps using the formula:

- 1250 'steps' per kilometer
- 2000 'steps' per mile

(V)    Group participation in Circle Canada can build camaraderie, as different offices or divisions, get together for friendly competition.

(VI)    The only equipment required is a pedometer. Some companies and organizations cover the complete cost of providing pedometers to employees, others subsidize pedometers and some provide them on a cost recovery basis. **Note:** I cannot stress strongly enough that it is **important to get accurate pedometers**. Unreliable pedometers can completely undermine the effectiveness of a program like Circle Canada or Route 66 and employees quickly lose interest.

(VII)    Data from Circle Canada can be managed within the company or provided on a monthly basis by the Speakwell staff.

(VIII)    The flexibility of Circle Canada means that it can be used by a two-person company or a 29,000-person company, such as Telus Telecommunications. The Wellness Division of the Telus Telecommunications Company were quick to see the value of Circle Canada as a company wide progam to help boost the activity level of their 29,000 employees. Telus has made pedometers available to their employees and, in conjunction with Speakwell, has created a designated portal where Telus employees can access Circle Canada and record their steps. What attracted Telus to Circle Canada was that every employee, wherever they were based, had equal access

Listen to Woody Guthrie's advice when he tells us that, *This land was made for you and me.*

Take a virtual walk in Canada or the USA (Circle Canada or Route 66).

*This land is your land, this land is my land,*
*From California to the New York Island*
*From the redwood forests to the gulf stream waters*
*This land was made for you and me.*

*This land is your land, this land is my land,*
*From Bonavista to Vancouver Island,*
*From the Arctic Circle to the Great Lake waters,*
*This land was made for you and me.*

Lyrics modified by The Travellers

Good luck as you go walking *that ribbon of highway.*

to this part of the company wellness plan. Each month they are provided with imformation about the walking activity of employees in different regions of the country. Circle Canada is available in both English and French. For more on walking as part of workplace wellness see Chapter 8.

The power of virtual walking is that you're no longer walking around the block or going to the corner store, you're on a journey that can take you through Toronto or Vancouver, St. Louis or San Bernadino and every city you pass through will bring you closer to your destination of High Level Wellness. Registration is easy, go to www.speakwell.com, hit the Circle Canada PED Step Log button, type in a username and password, (there's nothing to pay) and you're on your way to the journey of a lifetime.

The PED (Pedometer Enhancement Device) can be used by individuals and groups and provides:
- Daily step record
- Cumulative step totals
- Graphs of your progress
- Daily step average over a chosen time period
- Calories burned while walking
- Calories appropriate for weight maintenance
- BMI (Body Mass Index) calculator

*My doctor told me to stop having intimate dinners for four unless I invited three other people.*

Oscar Wilde

*I'd do anything to look like him, except exercise and eat right.*

Steve Martin

# 6

# Weight Loss and Weight Control

### The Calorie Story

The ebb and flow of calories will determine whether you're fat, very fat, thin, very thin or in true Goldilocks fashion, 'just right'. Calorie awareness is crucial and cannot be ignored. At school, we all heard the phrase *pay attention* and that's exactly what is required of you now, not just to the information in this chapter, but to the quality and quantity of calories you allow into your body.

Lance Armstrong not only recovered from cancer that spread from his testicles to his brain, but went on to become the greatest cyclist in the history of the Tour de France. Armstrong saw food as fuel, and while in hospital refused the hospital food, choosing instead to eat only high quality, carefully selected organic food. He felt he needed the highest quality nutrients to help him fight the disease which ravaged his body. In training, Armstrong knew precisely how many calories he burned on his bike, and carefully weighed his food so that his caloric intake matched his caloric output.

I'm not suggesting you become as intense as Lance Armstrong about nutrition. However, it makes sense to think carefully about the quality and quantity of fuel we give the only body we'll ever know.

My daughter lives in Australia and one of her friends,
a professional commedienne named Sue-Ann Post,
was overweight and diagnosed as a diabetic. Sue-Ann
devised her own diet and exercise regime.

*I had no desire to exercise in public. No power walking on the streets for me, or going to a gym where there might be (ugh) blondes in leotards. I had to find something that was cheap and close to home and I found salvation in my own backyard. Like many homes in the Brunswick/Coburg area, half my backyard consists of a great big slab of concrete. I looked at the concrete, looked at the back gate, and then paced out the distance. Approximately 20 metres. Ha, I thought, if I wasn't afraid of looking like an idiot I could just stroll up and down my garden a few dozen times and hell, that's half-a-kilometre walk right there. Fifty laps would be a kilometre.*

*It started to sound like a good idea. I began pacing up and down and fell into a comfortable rhythm. I did 50 comfortable, strolling laps and felt good. No strangers to deal with and never more than eight paces away from the loo, a glass of water, a chair, or someone to talk to. What can I say? I works for me.*

*I exercise almost every day. My friends laugh at me, call it the Pentridge Prison Yard Plan and whistle the theme of The Great Escape as I go, but I don't care. Sometimes I do figure-eights, sometimes I churn my arms as I walk, doing a bit of breast stroke or butterfly as I go. During the Olympics my girlfriend joined me in walking and we did tributes to other sports. We started from opposite ends of the yard, like pursuit bike racing, and tried to catch each other, and other stuff like that. My neighbors think we're insane, but that's neither here nor there, it works.*

(continued on page 94)

The calorie story is about the calories we burn when we move, the calories we take in with our food and drink and about the calories that are turned into fat and take up residence on our bodies. If you are interested in weight loss or weight control it makes life a lot easier if you understand the truth about calories. You can't manage your finances without knowing how much you earn and how much you spend and you can't manage your body weight without knowing something about the comings and goings of the calories in your life.

For example, most people have no idea how long it takes to work off or walk off the food they eat.

Once you understand the caloric content of food and drink and the sedentary nature of our society you cannot be surprised that we have been getting fatter and fatter every year. I believe we have reached the tipping point, when governments, health authorities, schools, magazines and newspapers and millions of individuals realize that enough is enough. This book will make its contribution to the common sense revolution of eating less, eating better and moving more.

### The Simple Truth About Calories

- A calorie is a unit of energy.
- We get our calories, and therefore our energy, from the food and drink we consume.
- In order to stay alive, our bodies are using energy (calories) every second of the day and night.
- The more we move the more calories we burn.
- The bigger we are the more calories we burn. This means that just to stay the same, a big person needs more calories than a small person. The stereotypical image is of skinny people who can eat anything and never put on weight because they have a 'high metabolism'. This is possible, but very unusual.
- As you lose weight (literally becoming smaller) you need a few less calories to maintain your weight. For every pound of weight you lose you need about 8 less calories per day. This fact is often overlooked and is one of the reasons that people regain weight when they 'go off their diet'.
- The word *metabolism* means the rate at which we burn calories. The metabolism of a slim adult man looks like this.

*So that's how I started regular exercise, and a few weeks in, I made the Big Discovery. I had started out somewhat grimly and reluctantly: "Just do the laps, burn off some calories, every little bit helps. You can do it." But then I started getting these endorphin rushes from exercise, and they're so cool. They lift your mood, give you a buzz, help you control your appetite and all because of a naturally produced drug in your body. How come the fitness fascists never mentioned that?*

*It's the opposite of a vicious circle. The exercise gives you a buzz, that makes you feel good, that helps cut down on your food intake, which helps you lose weight, which gives you a bigger buzz from the exercise. It's beautiful synergy. And I'm disturbed that we don't have a phrase in the English language for the opposite of vicious circle so I've coined one: a gruntled circle. Gruntled meaning happy, pleased and in good humor. Works for me. Let's build more of them.*

*So, that's what I did when I found out that I was diabetic, and the changes worked. I have lost 24 kilograms at last count and have dropped four clothes sizes. I have a neck, a waist and cheekbones. I have more energy and fewer black moods.*

*I can walk for hours and not feel at the end that someone has pounded the soles of my feet with a mallet. I cope with hot weather better. My periods are shorter, lighter and less painful (sorry guys, had to put that in for the ladies). I've rediscovered my ribs and other assorted bones that I thought had been lost for good.*

*But don't think for a moment that I've becomes some sick, skinny, waif type. Even with the weight loss, I'd still qualify for the super-heavyweight class in men's weightlifting, with a few kilos to spare.*

*The phrase I'm using at the moment is that I am skinny... like a bear. A big, healthy bear at that.*

|  | **Calories per hour** |
|---|---|
| Sleeping metabolism | 65 |
| (Often referred to as basal metabolism) | |
| Awake, lying still | 75 |
| Sitting at rest | 100 |
| (Resting metabolism) | |
| Walking slowly | 200 |
| (Exercise metabolism) | |
| Jogging (about 5.5 mph) | 600 |

If our slim man does nothing for 24 hours other than sleep, rest, sit and eat he will burn around 2000 calories. Two hundred of these calories are used to digest his food. So our slim adult male needs about 2000 calories to exist. A 120 lb female needs about 1800 calories to do the same. It takes more fuel to heat a big house than a small one so a heavy man or woman will burn more calories.

---

**Where Do The Calories Go?**

A typical picture of calorie use looks like this:

| 60-70% | Basal and Resting Metabolism |
|---|---|
| 10% | Digestion and processing of food |
| 20-30% | Movement and exercise |

The higher the percentage of your calories which are burned by movement and exercise the better.

---

The critical calorie zone is often between 2000 and 3000 calories. If we regularly have a muffin and a latte in the morning and maybe a chocolate bar for an 'energy boost' in the afternoon we are adding over 700 calories to our intake. Throw in a couple of alcoholic drinks and we will have consumed about half our basic 2000 survival calories and got very little value in terms of nutrition.

It's the daily habits that make the difference. An extra hundred calories seems like nothing until you start to look at it on a yearly basis.

*To lengthen thy life, lessen thy meals.*

Benjamin Franklin

*I guess I don't mind being old,
as I mind being fat and old.*

Benjamin Franklin

*People will accept your ideas much more readily if
you tell them they came from Benjamin Franklin.*

Benjamin Franklin

There are 365 days in a year. One pound of body fat is equal to 3500 calories. Therefore FOR EVERY EXTRA 10 calories you have on a daily basis you are consuming a pound's (0.45kg) worth of extra calories a year.

$$10 \text{ calories} \times 365 = 3650 \text{ calories}$$

Fortunately the body uses some energy to convert those calories to fat, but at least 1/2 of those extra calories will finish up as fat. Therefore, an extra 10 calories a day; 2 Smarties, 5 Tic Tacs or one stick of Wrigley's gum for example, will become 1/2 pound of fat a year.

---

While seeming to give you correct caloric information, many packaged food producers make it tricky to interpret by talking in terms of *serving size*. A 56 gram box of Smarties actually holds 56 Smarties, which we found by counting them. The 56 gram *serving size* is 256 calories, which means that **each individual Smartie is almost 5 calories.**
WHEN YOU THINK OF THIS IN TERMS OF STEPS, YOU WOULD HAVE TO WALK ABOUT THE LENGH OF A FOOTBALL FIELD TO *WALK OFF* ONE SMARTIE. IF YOU EAT ONE "SERVING SIZE" (A 56 GRAM BOX) YOU WILL NEED TO WALK NEARLY 3 MILES OR 4 1/2 KILOMETERS.
If weight control is a goal you can be your own *smartie* by leaving the boxes of multi-colored calories on the convenience store shelf.

---

Now think in terms of an extra 100 calories a day; a can of pop, 1/2 a chocolate bar or a piece of bread, and after one year you will be wearing an additional five or six pounds of fat. Little things mean a lot in love, life and weight control.

I've given you the bad news, but now for the good news. The more you move, the more you lose. For simplicity you can think of taking 20 steps to burn one calorie. So that if you record 10,000 steps on your pedometer, you've burned 500 calories. That might be all that it takes to be burning

*I don't want buns of steel,*
*I want cinnamon buns.*

Ellen de Generis

more calories than you consume. That might be all that it takes to be **losing** weight instead of **gaining** weight, or, just as important, **maintaining** weight.

You should be aware that the bigger you are the more calories you burn with each step.

A very big man who is over six feet tall and weights more than 300 lbs will need only 10 steps to burn one calorie. A tiny woman weighing 100lbs. or less and standing 4 ft 10 ins. tall will need 40 steps per calorie.

The following table provides a useful rough guide to convert your steps into calories, based on your weight and gender.

### Men

| Weight | Steps per Calorie |
|---|---|
| 150 lbs and under | 25 |
| 151 – 200 lbs | 20 |
| 201 – 250 lbs | 15 |
| 251 – 300 lbs | 10 |

### Women

| Weight | Steps per Calorie |
|---|---|
| 100 lbs and under | 40 |
| 101 – 110 lbs | 35 |
| 111 – 130 lbs | 30 |
| 131 – 150 lbs | 25 |
| 151 – 200 lbs | 20 |
| 201 – 250 lbs | 15 |
| 251 – 300 lbs | 12 |

If you require a more precise number, go to www.primusweb.com/fitnesspartner/ and click on "Activity Calorie Counter

People could look at the above table and think *I don't want to lose weight*

### Fidget Your Way to Fitness and Weight Loss
(Little moves mean a lot).

Dr. James Levine of the Mayo Clinic conducted an experiment on 20 sedentary adults, 10 of whom were obese and 10 of whom were close to normal weight. The two groups ate an identical number of calories from specially prepared foods. All the participants wore specially created undergarments with built in sensors, which recorded every wriggle, adjustment and movement. The 20 people were given identical tasks to perform during the day, and did no extra exercise.

The average difference in caloric expenditure between the thinner group and the heavy group was 350 calories per day. The thin group just didn't sit still, they adjusted positions, they stood up, walked around their desk, stretched and were rarely still for more than a few seconds. Their heavier counterparts were models of efficiency, wasting no energy or movement in the completion of a task.

That 350 calories a day can easily be the difference between fat and thin. Remember the math:

**350 calories a day x 365 days = 127,750 calories a year**

Divide that amount by 3500 to convert to pounds and you're looking at a 36 lb 16kg) difference. I'm not suggesting that you try to fidget your way thin but it is important that you never miss an opportunity to move and know that little things mean a lot.

The study findings so impressed Dr. Levine that he's redesigned his office so that his computer is mounted over a treadmill on which he walks at 0.7 miles per hour while he works. Dr. Levine notes, *The walking is addictive and terribly good fun.* He's received 40 requests from colleagues at Mayo for 'treadmill desks'. *Walking to work* has taken on a whole different meaning for Dr. Levine.

*because I'll have to walk further to burn calories if my weight goes down.* This is true, but it is not a good rationale for being overweight. Firstly, as we are informed daily in the popular media, being significantly overweight is unhealthy, affecting everything from A (arthritis) to Zzzzzz (quality of sleep). Secondly, muscle burns far more calories than fat and if we can lose fat and replace some of that lost weight with muscle we will become a far more efficient calorie burning machine. Thirdly, if you weigh 300 lbs it's not easy to walk much anyway and many very obese people become expert at minimizing the number of steps they take each day because of the effort and discomfort involved.

### Walking the Talk

I talk about walking and I write about walking because it works for me and millions of others. When I dress in the morning I put on my pedometer. I find the business of living provides me with about 5,000 steps, so in order to get to 10,000 and beyond I have to include a purposeful 45-minute walk as part of my day. I record my steps on the PED section of my web site (www.speakwell.com). You can do this too, or you can write them down in a notebook or calendar.

Two years ago, I recorded a total of 3,878,004 steps, an average of 10,624 per day. At 20 steps per calorie I burned 193,900 walking calories, which works out to 55 lbs (25kg) lost or not gained, 55lbs (25kg) that my body didn't have to process and store as fat. Last year my cumulative steps were 4,458,713.

**In simple terms, my walking program makes over 1 lb (0.45kg) per week difference to my life!!!**

### Completing the Calorie Story

Muscles are calorie burning machines and as you build muscle you increase your ability to burn calories and may well increase your overall metabolic rate. Sedentary North Americans typically lose 30% of their muscle mass in the 50 years between 20 and 70. About 1/2 lb of muscle disappears every year, at the same time fat is accumulating at many times that rate. This is the major reason why our metabolism slows as we age.

*Tomorrow is Fat Tuesday, and, of course, this being America, it will be followed by Even Fatter Wednesday, Obese Thursday and Morbidly Obese Friday.*

Jay Leno

*PLURES CRAPULA QUAM GLADIUS.*
*(Overeating kills more than the sword).*

Latin quote

This muscle loss can be offset by regular resistance training using free weights (bar bells and dumbbells), strength training machines or using your own body weight as resistance. [Chapter 11 provides an introduction to basic strength training]. The huge success of Curves is that it provides a structured, but informal, environment for women to work all the major muscle groups of the body within a 30-minute period. As a result, muscle mass is retained or increased, and inches and weight are decreased, particularly if the exercise program is combined with some form of caloric restriction.

Walking is good calorie burning exercise, but it doesn't do much for the muscles of the upper body. A balanced fitness program must include some regular resistance training to maintain or build muscle and enhance the body's calorie burning capacity. Movement burns calories and movement can build muscle, more muscle helps burn more calories in a wonderful positive spiral.

A major reason that is often cited against diets involving significant caloric restriction is that when you eat a lot less the **body's resting metabolic rate slows down** and you actually burn fewer calories at rest. This is a reality and is one of the reasons that weight loss is difficult (if it were easy we wouldn't have an obesity epidemic.) In a mechanism that goes back thousands of years, the body perceives a decreased caloric intake as a famine and slows down a little to try to conserve its integrity. This is another reason that it is important to move more during your diet, as exercise increases the metabolic rate and can help offset the lower resting metabolism. It also highlights the importance of a maintenance program when you have reached your ideal or target weight. Diets do work, but usually it's maintenance programs that fail.

One calorie burning part of exercise that is often overlooked is the increased metabolism that continues after you finish exercising. This is referred to as the post-exercise metabolism and means that the body continues to burn calories during the 'recovery' period after your workout. The more vigorous the exercise the more calories are burned after its completion.

## Top 10 Walking Songs

1. Walk Like a Man        (4 Seasons)
2. I Go Walking After Midnight (Patsy Cline)
3. I'm Walking        (Fats Domino)
4. I'm Walking on Sunshine (Katrina and the Waves)
5. Walk Right In        (Rooftop Singers)
6. These Boots are Made for Walking (Nancy Sinatra)
7. I Walk the Line        (Johnny Cash)
8. Walk Like an Egyptian        (The Bangles)
9. Walk Right Back        (Everly Brothers)
10. Walk On By        (Dionne Warwick)

Note: Given what happened in New Orleans, there's something oddly prophetic about an 80's group called *Katrina and the Waves.*

## Calorie Facts That You Might Overlook

All types of food are not created equal.

1 g of carbohydrate has 4 calories
1 g of protein has 4 calories
1 g of fat has 9 calories!

Per unit of weight, fat has more than twice the calories of carbohydrate and protein.

The news about fat gets worse. In order to convert dietary fat into body fat, the body needs to **expend** only 2.5 calories to **store** 100 fat calories. It's easy for the body to store the fat in your diet as body fat. However, in order to convert and store 100 calories of dietary protein or carbohydrate as fat the body must use 23 calories, nearly 10 times the amount it uses to store an equal amount of fat.

If it's available the body will always choose to store fat rather than carbohydrate or protein. The obvious message is to be very selective about the fat you choose to consume, especially if you are trying to lose weight.

## Wonderful Web Sites

### Activity Calorie Calculators

To show the caloric cost of various activities based on your body weight would mean pages and pages of tables in this book. Fortunately, there are some excellent web sites, which provide accurate caloric information, taking into account the type and duration of the activity and your body weight.

One useful site is The Fitness Jumpsite at www.primusweb.com/fitnesspartner/. Once there, click on the "activity calorie calculator" and you can have access to the caloric cost of 158 different activities based on your own body weight.

A similar service is provided by A.D.A.M. at http://avera.adam.com/pages/tools/cal_burn.htm This site provides the calorie cost of a wide range of recreational and sporting activities.

*I'd rather be thin than famous.*

Jack Kerouac

*Dieting can be the triumph of mind over platter.*

Unknown

### The Caloric Content of Food and Beverages

A web site, which will be very useful to you in checking the calories in familiar foods, can be found at www.calorieking.com/. This site has a database of over 40,000 foods, but the outstanding feature involves fast food and can be accessed by clicking on *Create a Meal*. Using excellent graphics you can get complete caloric information from any combination of meals available at leading fast food franchises including McDonalds, Pizza Hut and Starbucks. Because this is web based it can be constantly updated to keep pace with new products.

A web site, which combines both nutritional and caloric information of foods and beverages along with the caloric cost of exercise, can be found at www.fitday.com. This site enables you to set weight loss goals and then track your progress numerically and visually in the form of graphs and charts. The site is packed with information and is a good example of effective use of web-based technology. It's not for everyone, but for those who are analytical and hungry for information, it's Nirvana.

### So You Really, Really Want to Lose Weight!!

This section is not for people who need to *lose a few pounds* or people who want to *firm up a little*, this section is for people with a body mass index (BMI) well in excess of 30 (to calculate your BMI go to www.speakwell.com, click the **PED Step Log** button, create an account [no charge], sign in and go to **tools** on the bar displayed at the top of the page.) This is for people who are not just overweight, but obese.

The conventional wisdom is that crash diets crash, that people who lose weight fast, gain it back faster and that rapid weight loss is the gateway to *yo-yo syndrome* of *lose weight, gain weight* (often referred to as *the rhythm method of girth control*). Many academics teach that people gain weight gradually and therefore should lose weight gradually. It sounds right, but my observations tell me otherwise. People who have to lose 50, 60, 70, 80, 90, 100 lbs (23, 27, 32, 36, 41, 45kg) or more are **unlikely to be successful** walking a bit more each day and modifying the size of their portions at mealtimes. This sounds like heresy, especially in a book about walking, but it happens to be the truth.

107

*A great pleasure in life is doing what people say you cannot do.*

Walter Gagehot

*We tend to eyeball what we want to eat and drink, dish it up and then mindlessly eat while we carry on a conversation or read a newspaper. The cue that we are finished eating is that our food is gone.*

Brian Wansink

*Food is an important part of a balanced diet.*

Fran Lebowitz

If I had 50 lbs (23kg) or more to lose (and maybe much less) I would enter a program of rigorous caloric restriction. I would certainly combine this with an incremental walking program and upper body exercise, but the key to my weight loss would be keeping my caloric intake way down.

---

### It's hard to lose a lot of weight by exercise alone.

Do you want to lose 3/4 lb (0.35kg)? It's easy, just run, or even walk, a marathon. A marathon is just over 26 miles (41 plus kilometers). You'll actually lose quite a bit more than 3/4 lb (.035kg) when you add in sweat loss, but that will all come back when you re-hydrate.

### Let's run the numbers.

1 mile is approximately 2000 steps. At 20 steps per calorie you are burning 100 calories per mile (about 65 calories per kilometer).

$$26 \text{ miles} \times 100 \text{ calories} = 2600 \text{ calories}$$

It takes 3500 calories to burn one pound (0.45kg) of weight. So, as you can see, you will need to add another 9 miles (14.5km) to your marathon to burn off one pound (0.45kg) of weight.

---

Don't be too discouraged by the above example, you don't need to run marathons, although part of your weight loss program must involve movement. If you record 10,000 steps per day on your pedometer, this is the equivalent of covering 5 miles (8km) at 2000 steps per mile (1250 steps per km). If you average 10,000 steps per day for a week, that's 35 miles (56km) walking each week, way longer than a marathon and just about 1 lb (0.45kg) of fat burned. **The key is creating daily habits of movement.**

### On Your Marks, Get Set, Get Set, Get Set

First, ask yourself the question, *Do I really, really want to lose weight?* If you're not sure, don't expect to be successful. If your mind is full of 'maybes' and qualifying thoughts, the chances are you're looking for a

### The Devil Made Me Do It

God created man and woman in his own image and they were lean and fit.

Satan said, *I know how I can get back in this game.*

God brought forth fruit and vegetables of many colours packed with nutrients so man/woman could live long, healthy lives.

Satan created fast food and brought forth the monster burgers and the 99¢ cheeseburger and Satan said to man, *You want fries with that?* And man said, *Yea! Supersize them.* And gained 5 lbs.

And God created low-fat yogurt that woman might keep the figure which man found so fair.

Satan brought forth high fat ice cream and woman gained weight.

God said, *Try my salad.*

And Satan created creamy salad dressing and chocolate for dessert.

And God created olive oil for cooking.

Satan countered with beef fat for deep-frying. Man gained many pounds and his cholesterol went through the roof.

God produced running shoes so that people might move and be slim.

Satan brought forth cable TV and remote controls. People gained 20 more pounds.

God said, *You're running up the score, Satan* and created the humble, healthy potato.

Satan removed the skin, deep fried the potato and made chips.

And people clutched their remote controls, ate their chips and Satan saw and said, *This is good.*

loophole rather than setting yourself up for success. In Corinthians we're told, *If the trumpet have an uncertain sound, who shall gird him/herself to battle?*

Listed below are typical negative thought patterns you might have to deal with before launching into the weight loss phase of your diet.

10. *I tried and failed before.*

    Remember this is true about almost every breakthrough in our society. It is reported that Edison *failed* 10,000 times before creating a successful light bulb.

9. *Diets are boring and I deserve some fun in my life.*

    It's a lot easier to have fun if you're slim and active and have plenty of energy.

8. *It doesn't seem fair that my spouse eats as much as I do and doesn't gain weight.*

    Remember, life isn't always 'fair'.

7. *I can't go on a diet unless my wife/husband/boyfriend does it with me.*

    This takes the responsibility away from you and allows you to blame someone else.

6. *With my travel commitments and social life it's difficult to say 'no' to the food and drink I'm offered.*

    People will respect you for it.

5. *I've got a slow metabolism.*

    If this is true, which it probably isn't, it doesn't prevent you losing weight, but just makes it a bit harder.

4. *Low calorie foods don't taste good.*

    This is not true, they might be less fatty and sugary but your taste buds quickly adjust.

    *On a personal note, some years back I switched from whole milk to low fat milk. Initially the low fat milk tasted 'chalky' and insipid, but now it's whole milk that just doesn't have the right taste and feel on my re-educated taste buds.

3. *I'll start in the spring when I can get out more.*
   *I'll start my diet when I've finished this project.*
   *I'll start soon – later - in June - on January 1ˢᵗ - when I get out of this relationship etc. etc.*

    As George Allen once said, *The future is now!*

2. *It's easy to go from a diet to an eating disorder.*

    Millions of people diet, but only a very small percentage develop an eating disorder. The origin of most eating disorders is psychological

### Starting on Monday

*Starting on Monday I'm living on carrots and bouillon,*
*Starting on Monday I'm bidding the doughnut adieu*
*I'm switching from After Eight Mints to afternoon Rye Crisp*
*And people will say, "Can that skinny person be you?"*
*Starting on Monday I will be strong*

*Starting on Monday I'll run for a mile in the morning*
*That's after push-ups, sit-ups and touching my toes*
*The gratification that I once used to find in lasagna*
*I'll find in the song of a bird, the scent of a rose*
*Starting on Monday I will be strong*

*But Tuesday friends came by and they brought homemade muffins*
*Wednesday I had to stop jogging because of my back*
*Thursday I read in the paper that an excess of egg yolk*
*Would clog up my vessels and probably cause an attack*

*Saturday evening I went with my kids to a movie*
*I begged for a Perrier ™ but all they would serve me was shakes*
*Sunday my stomach oozed over my waistband*
*And filled with self-loathing I sought consolation in cakes*

*But, starting on Monday my will will be stronger than brownies*
*Anything more than a celery stick will seem crude*
*The bones in my pelvis will make their initial appearance*
*A testament to my relentless abstention from food*
*Starting on Monday, I'll be the same.*

Music and lyrics by Martin Collis

and has little to do with practical caloric restriction.

1.      David Letterman's Number 1 reason for not starting a diet.
*If I do lose weight, I'll only gain it back.*

You can find plenty of experts who will validate that thought. The often-quoted Albert J Stunkard, MD stated. *Most obese people do not stay in treatment.....of those who stay in treatment most will not lose weight and of those who do lose weight, most will regain it.* How would you like Albert Stunkard for a coach? *Well they nearly always beat us, and if we do happen to beat them, it will just encourage them to train harder and beat us even worse next year.*

I prefer the thinking of the old Ohio State football coach, Woody Hayes, who, at a team breakfast said, *Men, you've just got your eggs and your bacon. The way I see it is the chicken made a contribution, but the pig made a commitment.* Without a real commitment it's very unlikely you will lose weight and keep it off. If you make a well-planned commitment you can take great delight in proving Dr. Albert (why wasn't he called Jeremiah?) Stunkard wrong. **We are each an experiment of one**, we are each unique and we each have the ability to face up to challenges and difficulties and emerge successful. **Each and every one of us really is a walking miracle**.

### Losing It

There are more books written about food than there are about sex and it's easy to feel overwhelmed by the sheer volume of, often conflicting, information. If we want to lose weight, which approach do we take? Low fat? High protein? Low carbohydrate? Food combinations? The Glycemic Index? Vegetarian? Or do we select one of the thousands of weight loss books, some of which are weird and some outright dangerous?

When I studied many of the leading diets I found that they averaged a little under 1600 calories a day. Currently, a typical North American male averages a caloric intake just under 3000 calories a day, while women consume around 2500 calories. Regardless of the name of the diet, **if you suddenly start taking in 1000 – 1500 fewer calories each day you will lose weight!!** Recent research has found that after one to two years there was no statistical difference between people who followed different dietary paths. If they stayed with their diet, whether it was Atkins, The Zone or Ornish they lost about the same amount of weight.

*Oh, that this too too solid flesh would melt,*
*thaw and resolve itself into a dew.*

Hamlet

William Shakespeare

The simple truth is that **if you follow a sustained and significant reduction of caloric intake you will lose weight. If you return to old eating and lifestyle patterns you will regain the weight!!**

Diets are a bit like running shoes, if you find one that works for you stay with it. I did an extensive review of major diets titled 'The Great Diet Debate', in the Fall 2002 edition of my newsletter, *Well,* which can be reviewed online at http://www.speakwell.com/well/2002_fall/1a.shtml.

If you feel that social support is important to you, then groups such as Weight Watchers (http://www.weightwatchers.com/) or TOPS (Take Off Pounds Sensibly) http://www.tops.org/ might be good choices. If you like to use your computer, eDiets has some well-structured programs (http://www.ediets.com/). Dr. Dean Ornish lays out a complete program, with vegetarian recipes from leading chefs along with exercise and meditation. You can lose weight successfully if you follow the popular South Beach Diet, and even Dr. Atkins' diet, if you read it carefully, will provide a path to weight loss, which, after the first few weeks, provides enough vegetables (*if you're not eating vegetables, you're not on the Atkins Diet*) and encouragement to exercise.

Why write so much about weight loss in a walking book?

(I)   One of the reasons two thirds of the population are overweight or obese is because movement, and particularly walking, have become less and less a part of their daily lives.
(II)  Walking is a natural, inexpensive way to help lose weight and is often **vital in keeping weight off.**
(III) Walking is a healthy, mind expanding activity and wellness is the ultimate goal of this book.

### The Heavy Cost of Heaviness

Nobody (that's no body) enjoys being overweight, which places a strain on every organ in the body. In a study of obese people who resorted to surgery in order to lose weight, nearly all said they'd rather have a major handicap such as deafness, legal blindness, psoriasis or even amputation than be fat again. Every single person said they'd rather have their standard of living at a healthy weight than to be an obese millionaire.

**Signs You Don't See at Hospital Reception**

**NO FAULT OF
THEIR OWN
WARD
←**

**THEY DID IT
TO THEMSELVES
WARD
→**

*Let your head be more than a
funnel to your stomach.*

German Proverb

*To eat is a necessity, but to eat
intelligently is an art.*

La Rochefoucauld

The primary reasons to lose weight and be active are positive; you want to have a feeling of control, be energetic, to look good and to enjoy life. But if that's not enough for you, just remember all the negative things that are associated with overweight and obesity. It's a frightening list:

Diabetes (The link between diabetes and obesity is so strong that it has led to a new word "diabesity". Four of the most undesirable conditions associated with diabetes are: Amputation, Blindness, Kidney Failure, Impotence.)

-High Blood Pressure
-Stroke
-Heart Disease
-Sleep Apnea
-Depression
-Kidney Disease
-Osteoarthritis
-Glaucoma
-Alzheimer's Disease
-Fibromyalgia
-Chronic Fatigue
-Sexual Dysfunction
-Congestive Heart Failure
-Gallbladder Disease
-Abdominal Hernias
-Varicose Veins
-Liver Problems
-Asthma
-Gout
-Hyperlipidemia
- Back Pain (Particularly low back pain)

Cancer (Women) -Uterus
-Gallbladder
-Cervix
-Ovaries
-Breast
-Colon

Cancer (Men) -Prostate
-Colo-Rectal

Not surprisingly, having seen the above list, overweight and obesity will shorten your life. All you have to gain from diet and exercise is a healthier, less painful, longer life.

Obesity is a preventable condition, except in a few cases, that can have a negative impact on our sleep, sexual performance, employability, energy level, vision, memory and can be a major contributing factor in the likelihood that we will suffer from one or more chronic diseases.

If it were possible to sentence criminals to be fat, or to carry 50lb sacks of flour 24 hours a day, it would be struck down as a cruel and unusual punishment. Only we can sentence ourselves to be fat, as Shakespeare said, *I am my own executioner.* So of course I want you to walk away from your weight problems and of course I want to make sense of the calories you consume. No ice cream, no chocolate, no French fries, no cheesecake, no mocha with whipped cream is worth a lifetime of dragging around extra pounds. As one physician, who is an expert in weight loss, never tires of telling his patients, *You think going without dessert is 'hard', you tell me giving up martinis is 'hard'. I'll tell you what 'hard' is: 'hard' is a heart attack, 'hard' is a stroke where part of your body is paralyzed, 'hard' is living the rest of your life with diabetes.*

### Leaning Towards the Hare, Not the Tortoise

There are many reasons to lose weight **fast.** A powerful psychological reason is that you quickly start to get positive feedback from family, friends and co-workers. For example, if you have 65 lbs (30 kg) to lose and in a period of a few weeks you lose 25 lbs (11 kg), you start hearing:

> *You're looking good!*
> *You've lost weight!*
> *Are you in love?*
> *I wish I had your will power.*

Comments which are music to the ears.

However, if you are less rigorous but still eat carefully, cutting down on alcohol, candy, desserts and a number of other favorites and try to increase your daily exercise and after 6 weeks have lost a very commendable 5 lbs (2.25kg), nobody will notice!! Nobody will say how well you're doing, your

*You've come too far in life to take orders from a cookie.*

Stephen Gullo
*Thin Tastes Better*

*A quotation at the right moment is like bread to the famished.*

The Talmud

elasticized clothes will still leave 'wounds' when you take them off and you'll start to question whether all the restrictions are worth it.

Psychologically it's much easier to **cut out,** rather than **cut down.** You have clarity and certainty and there's no room for debate about the occasional fast food meal, cocktail, candy bar or desert. Ambiguity is the devil's volleyball and if you're hungry and uncertain, before you know it you'll have eaten 1000 useless calories.

In 2001, James Anderson MD, who is one of North America's leading weight loss and diabetes experts, reviewed the results of 29 studies involving thousands of people who lost weight with various forms of caloric restriction. Anderson's meta-analysis not only looked at how people lost weight, but whether the weight loss was sustained. He published the results in the American Journal of Clinical Nutrition and one of his key findings was, ***There just isn't evidence that slow weight loss results in better maintenance of weight loss than that obtained from very low calorie diets.***

### Losing It Yourself

Ten Commandments (or strong suggestions):

1. **Positive Self-Talk.** Your self-talk should tell you that you are setting out to give yourself one of the most important gifts you can ever receive, the gift of life. You are not being punished; you are merely shaping your lifestyle so that you and your body can be all that they can be.
2. **Align your attitude.** Make a commitment and be prepared to stay with it. You are going to eat carefully and eat only healthy, nutritious foods. There are no exceptions, no loopholes.
3. **No alcohol.** Whether it's beer, wine or liquor, there's more than 100 calories a glass and the problem with alcohol is that one drink often leads to another. Also, alcohol often seems to give you permission to eat chips and other junk food.
4. **Just for fun; no 'C' foods.** Calorie is a 'C' word and you can cut out plenty by just removing 'C' foods from your life. For a complete list go to http://www.speakwell.com/well/2003fall/c.shtml. Examples include: Cake (remember muffins are cake by another name),

*Our bodies are apt to be
our autobiographies.*

Gelett Burgess

*What would you attempt to do
if you knew you could not fail?*

Dr. Robert Schuller

most commercial cereals, crackers, cookies, croissants, chips, candy, chocolate, crepes, crumpets, carbonated drinks, convenience foods and comfort foods. The phrase 'common sense' also starts with 'C', so, of course, you can include some of the 'high C's' such as chicken (grilled or poached), celery and cabbage. This is obviously just a little gimmick but it will provide consistent reminders to go the distance with your diet. Lastly, carbohydrate is another big 'C' word, and although there are plenty of nutritious carbs, there's a lot more refined carbs that will sabotage your weight loss program.

5.  **No Special Occasions.** Once you start making exceptions, you're in trouble, because our lives can be full of 'special occasions' or extenuating circumstances where the thing to do is eat and drink. Be social, be polite and be kind, and don't have that 'healthier than thou' attitude. If you are pressured by someone, just say your doctor put you on a restricted diet for a while. So stay with your program on birthdays, football Sundays, when friends come by, at business lunches, at TGIF coffee breaks, at conference socials, on plane trips, at weddings and the hundred and one other events that come with food and drink. It won't be long before you reach your goal and there will be plenty of room in your maintenance program to eat and drink socially. Oprah, for whom I have a lot of respect, has a creative way of dealing with the 'special occasion' loophole. In her program "12 Weeks to a Better Body", she allows up to 3 days when you can deviate moderately from your diet. These must be **nominated in advance** and might be something such as an anniversary, birthday or reunion, where you can have a glass or two of wine or piece of cake without feeling guilty. I can buy into that, but would suggest that the 'special occasions' don't exceed once a month. One other Oprah suggestion that I like is, "You must stop eating three hours before bedtime."

6.  **Beware of brand names and processed food.** In an era of mergers and multinational companies most of the famous brand name foods are manufactured by conglomerates who have no interest in your weight or your health and whose only goal is to make money. There's not a big profit margin marketing fresh fruits and vegetables so they'll sell you products in packages,

YOUR LOST WEIGHT

*"Ready to head back?"*

*Fat cells retreat. They don't go away. They collapse like a balloon and wait for their next opportunity to attack. Fat cells are hungry, ambitious, resilient, patient and very, very proud.*

Remar Sutton

cans and boxes that are great for shelf life but not so good for self-life. Labeling is often misleading and is full of words such as 'less', 'low', 'light', 'reduced', 'vitamin enriched' and health related terminology. Bear in mind that one of the reasons we have an obesity epidemic is that we've been persuaded by advertising of those corporations to eat more than we need, so don't look for salvation from the people who helped you put on the weight in the first place. For further reading on this subject, read *Fast Food Nation* by Eric Schlosser, *Fat Land* by Greg Critser, *The Omnivore's Dilemma* by Michael Pollan and *Don't Eat This Book* by Morgan Spurlock.

> Multi-level, multi-national companies are money machines, which only make sense to stockholders and number crunchers. They make no sense looked at from a health perspective. The same company might sell calorie dense junk food along with weight loss programs and products, or sport drinks and cigarettes.

7. **Keep Moving.** *Walk on, walk on with hope in your heart* and never miss a chance to move. In many ways a calorie burned by exercise is better than a calorie that you save by not eating. Movement maintains or builds muscle and muscles burn calories. Inside muscle cells are what's called mitochondria, which are known as the 'powerhouses' or 'energy factories' of the body. The mitochondria help break down the fuel from food and turn it into energy the body can use. The more muscle you have, the more mitochondria are available to turn food into energy, which in turn enables us to burn more calories.

8. **Eat in.** The more people in North America have eaten outside the home, the fatter they have become. At home you have total control of menu, portion size and ingredients. If you **do** eat out you have to make good choices. Do the simple things such as having an appetizer instead of an entrée, or split an entrée with a friend or to take home for a later meal. Don't look at the dessert

*Accept the diagnosis, defy the prognosis.*

Nancy Wardle

The old saying went:

*Eat, drink and be merry for tomorrow you die.*

But mostly you don't die, you wake up and
you're obese.

*Eat, drink and be wary.*

Martin Collis

menu. Just remember you are paying to be served and don't feel intimidated and try to impress the waiter. If all you want is a salad with dressing on the side (a must) don't feel you have to eat the roll or order something else. **Avoid fast food outlets, period.** I know you can get an indifferent salad at McDonalds and I know Jared lost weight by eating at Subway (he must have done a ton of exercise) but going to a fast food place to lose weight is like going to an orgy just for the grapes, it doesn't make sense.

9.  **Vitamin Supplements.** If you're eating plenty of organic fruits and vegetables you are going a long way to providing the body with the nutrients and vitamins it needs. It's worth noting that organic produce typically contains more vitamins than non-organic. If you are not a vegetarian, fish such as tuna, salmon and sardines are an excellent source of Omega-3, which is one of the essential fatty acids shown to play a significant role in preventing heart disease. Omega-3 fatty acids are also found in deep green vegetables and some grains and seeds, particularly flax seed. Another essential fatty acid is Omega-6, which is important in supporting the body's immune system and in suppressing inflammation. Omega-6 fatty acids are abundant in olive oil, canola oil, avocados and many grains. Essential fatty acids get their name because they are essential in your diet, as the body can't manufacture them. Our species has survived for years without taking vitamin supplements but for peace of mind while dieting it is probably advisable to take the following: One good multi-vitamin daily, containing a full range of B vitamins.

    > 1000 mg of vitamin C
    > 1000 mg of Omega-3
    > 500 mg of Omega-6

    To learn more about supplements, read *The Vitamin Revolution* by Michael Janson MD and *Fats That Heal, Fats That Kill* by Dr. Udo Erasmus.

10. **Avoid extreme behaviors.** Fanatical dieting and fanatical exercising are bad for your body, your health and your social life. In your self-directed program don't allow your caloric intake to dip below 1200 per day. Remember that injury and intensity often go together in exercise, which is one of many reasons why

**A few favorite acronyms**

TRUST  - Tomorrow's Results Ultimately Start Today

Lynn Beecroft

FAITH  - Find Answers In The Heart

Lynn Beecroft

FEAR     - Future Expectations, Awful Repercussions

PLAY     - Put Leisure Around You

SPA       - Simply Pay Attention

WELL     -Walk Everyday, Live Longer

Guy LeMesurier

The MELLOW formula for high-level wellness

       M- Magic of the mind

       E- Exercise

       L- Laughter

       L- Love

       O- Optimal nutrition

       W- Wonder

BOTSWANA

    - Bald On Top, Spreading Waistline and Narrowing Arteries

MADD     - Mothers Against Drunk Driving

DAM       - Mothers Against Dyslexia

The HAWAII wellness formula

       H - Humble (remember, ego eats brains)

       A - Accepts change

      W - Wellness oriented

       A - Action oriented (Just do it)

       I - Intuitive (Trust your gut, it's very well informed)

       I - Inventive (Seek creative solutions to problems)

ACRONYM -A Crazy Reminder Of Names You Misplaced or Annoyingly Cryptic References Of Names You Make

walking is important, as it's usually injury free. A weight loss of about 10 lbs a month can be a realistic, safe and rewarding goal for your self-directed diet. (See Chapter 15 *The Power of Fifteen*)

### Maintenance

**You must have an exit strategy, which is your maintenance program.** Plan how you are going to live your exercise and eating life once you have achieved your weight loss goal. Walking 10,000 steps per day and more could be the foundation of your maintenance. Walking gets easier with every pound and kilogram you lose.

Remember, the word **diet** comes from the Greek word **diatia,** which means PRESCRIBED WAY OF LIVING, **not** restricted calories. Your maintenance program is you real diet, your way of living, your lifestyle. You've broken some destructive habits in order to lose weight and it makes no sense to return to them. If you do what you've always done you'll be what you've always been. To practice the old behaviors and expect to be different is a form of insanity.

Now is the time for moderation, to raise a glass with friends, to savor your favorite foods, always remembering *Enough is abundance to the wise* and that the wise realize that *Nothing is enough for the person for whom enough is too little.*

Perhaps that great philosopher Tom Petty summarized the modern American way of eating and living when he sang *Too much, ain't enough.* That's what got two thirds of us overweight, but you are not one of them any more.

---

The caloric restriction phase of your diet is a tightrope, where a miss-step can have you wobbling or falling off. The ongoing maintenance phase is a sidewalk where you have more flexibility and choices, but still don't want to go off the path and on to the road.

---

*Red meat's not bad for you.
Now blue-green meat, that's bad for you!*

Tommy Smothers

*My uncle in Texas thought that a
vegetarian was someone who ate
vegetables with their meat.*

Joe Ely

## Afterword

This is **your** weight loss program based on **your** priorities, **your** timetable, **your** personality and **your** needs. One size doesn't fit all. Be realistic and disciplined and remember the words of Steven Covey, *Make a promise, and keep it.* If you approach your weight loss armed with knowledge, determination and a positive attitude, it just might turn into one of the easiest, hard things you've ever done.

## MEDICALLY SUPERVISED WEIGHT LOSS

Scientists are still looking for a weight loss medication where the side-effects (e.g. anal leakage) don't outweigh the benefits. Every major drug company is aiming to produce the holy grail of a drug, which will help you lose weight with minimum effort. Of course, we already have the Holy Grail, it's called exercise, which helps you lose weight and has only positive side effects. That's why my company, Speakwell, markets a line of pedometers in pill bottles.

**Wellness Prescription**

Dosage: Take 10,000 steps daily.
Caution: Can be habit forming.
Side Effects: Will cause weight loss,
wellness and feelings of euphoria.
Active Ingredient: You

R̲ₓ Not available as a pill or suppository!
Website: www.speakwell.com

I'd suggest you don't wait around for the wonder drug; it might be a very long wait.

### Surgical Procedures

Invasive surgery is not really in the purview of this book. The technique known as 'stomach stapling' is quite high profile, as celebrities such as Carnie Wilson and Al Roker have undergone the procedure. This is a last resort operation for morbidly obese people for whom no other program has worked. Essentially, the surgeon creates a tiny pouch, which is your

North Americans

*Eat more*
*Eat badly*
*Eat out*
*Eat fast*

None of the above are conducive
to health or weight control.

To mis-quote Shakespeare,
*We need the taming of the chew.*

new stomach. This restricts eating to 1 to 3 oz (85 grams) of food at a time, and if you exceed that, you regurgitate in a fairly drastic form of negative feedback. A friend of mine has undergone the surgery and hates the eating restrictions, but loves the fact that she has lost more than 1/2 her body weight, can fit in airplane seats, can sleep properly and for the first time in years is walking regularly.

Liposuction is a Hollywood operation that has become mainstream. Google comes up with almost two million references, many of which include pictures of slim, tanned, supposedly post liposuction patients. I'm sure there are people for whom liposuction might be an important and justifiable procedure, but I believe they are in the minority. For most people it is a loophole, a get slim quick scheme. Like any surgical procedure, liposuction is not without risk, death is very rare, but infection is always possible, as is seroma, which is a pooling of oozing bodily fluid. Swelling, bruising and locally painful areas are an almost guaranteed side effect and for many procedures you can expect to lose a week or more off work.

If you undergo liposuction in order to lose weight, unless you make big post surgical changes to your lifestyle, the weight you have removed will return. It makes more sense to make the lifestyle changes first and bypass the surgery.

As usual, Dave Barry enables us to laugh at ourselves with his off center look at liposuction.

*In fact, many of us are willing to consider extreme measures to become slimmer. I bet that more than once, when nobody was around, you've grabbed a handful of your fat and wished something truly ridiculous, something like: "I wish some doctor would just stick a tube into my body and turn on a pump and suck this fat right out: Ha ha! You crazy nut! What a wacky idea! Do you honestly think, with all the serious medical problems confronting the human race, that a physician-a person who has gone through long, grueling years of medical training in order to acquire vital healing skills that could be used to make a real difference in the lives of suffering people-do you honestly think that such a person would use this precious ability to suck bacon cheeseburgers out of your thighs?*

*Well, certainly not for free. No sir, it could run you more than a thousand buckaroos per thigh. This is not because the liposuction procedure itself is difficult. The*

*There is nothing noble in being superior to someone else. The true nobility is in being superior to your previous self.*

Hindu proverb

*The highest reward for a person's toil is not what they get for it, but what they become by it.*

John Ruskin

*procedure itself could be performed flawlessly by anyone who has completed the basic training course at Roto-Rooter.*
[Excerpt taken from *Dave Barry Turns 40*, published by Ballantine Books]

### The Bernstein Diet

A rapid weight loss program with which I am familiar is the one created by Stanley Bernstein, MD, who has studied bariatric (weight related) medicine for over 30 years. Dr. Bernstein has over 50 clinics in Canada and now in the USA. http://www.drbdiet.com/as/menu/mb:Home

His approach is an unusual one in our permissive society, in that clients are expected to stick closely to his balanced, very low calorie diet and if they don't, they are given a couple of warnings, after which they are politely asked to leave the program. It's refreshing to see a commercial clinic that will not take your money if you're deviating from the prescribed dietary lifestyle. Every clinic is staffed with a physician and nurses, urine is checked weekly to see if clients are metabolizing fat. Dr. Bernstein describes his diet as follows.

*It's a low-fat, restricted carbohydrate diet with a normal amount of protein, with oral vitamins and minerals and it involves injectable B vitamins. It also involves behavioral modification techniques.*

Patients attend the clinic three times a week for weigh-ins, food diary assessments, urinalysis, injections and counseling.

Patients can expect to lose between four and five pounds per week, or 16 to 20 pounds per month. In addition to the dramatic weight loss, the thing that excites the physicians who work with the program is the number of patients that they take off medication.

The major key to the program is the medical supervision, Bernstein says. *We evaluate patients for medical associations like thyroid disease, diabetes, hypertension, sleep apnea and many others. We are able to manage these diseases with the weight loss.* When patients get to their weight goal they are encouraged to stay with a structured maintenance program, which is offered at a nominal cost.

*Effort is the one strictly un-derived and original contribution we make to the world. Many things are given to us health, talent, abilities, but effort is the element **we** can add.*

George Sheehan

*The most important block is not the one you walk, but the one inside your head that whispers you* can't do it, *or* you'll never be slim.

Martin Collis

On the subject of exercise, Bernstein points out that, *Many can't exercise in the first place because they are ill or have too much excess weight. They can't start exercising until they lose some weight. We encourage exercise when appropriate.*

### The Multi-Billion Dollar Question

Given the fact that obesity is the cause of so much death and disease in North America it has been ironic that, except in exceptional cases, obesity itself was not a treatable problem that would be covered by insurance companies and health care plans. One could only get treatment for the problems caused by obesity such as high blood pressure, diabetes or heart disease. (This is like treating someone for loss of blood and ignoring the fact that the hemorrhage has been caused by a knife or bullet.)

There are signs that this might be beginning to change. In 2005, Medicare in the USA has stated that it now may be possible to treat obesity before it leads to illness, in effect, declaring that obesity itself is an illness requiring medical attention.

Medicare will also consider reimbursement for obesity treatment options other than surgery, such as membership in a weight loss program. Not unreasonably, Medicare will require evidence concerning the "effectiveness" of any treatment before it pays up. At present they haven't laid out criteria for an *effective* treatment, so it will be a while before people can benefit from this plan. It will be interesting to watch insurance companies and governments deal with the medicalization of obesity.

My short-term advice is not to wait for a pill, a procedure or a government program. If you are overweight or obese, now is the time to start losing it.

## Final Thoughts

If you are morbidly obese and unable to move very much, or if you are considering really rapid weight loss, you would be well advised to initiate your weight loss under carefully medically supervised conditions. Many hospitals offer weight loss programs, particularly in the States. Be careful to select a program with a good track record where information and assistance are readily available.

*I give you bitter pills in sugar coating. The pills are harmless; the poison is in the sugar.*

Stanislaw Lec

*As a nation we are food illiterates whose diet has changed more in the past 40 years than it did in the previous 40,000.*

Unknown

For a detailed look at my unique program for weight loss, weight control and high level mind/body functioning see Chapter 15, *The Power of Fifteen.*

### Walk your way to peace of mind

*I grew up thinking never to be late. Run if you have to. Wolf down your breakfast. Run downstairs. Press the button repeatedly for an elevator which doesn't arrive fast enough, or get into a frenzy waiting in long lines at the supermarket.*

*I spent my time running after time without ever stopping.*

*Then I switched to walking, which has saved my life. Walking permits me to think, to mature, to go naturally forward instead of trying to force things my way.*

*Walking opens doors towards wisdom and imagination.*

*Walking, let me say it out loud, leads to happiness.*

*And don't you think that I exaggerate! If you feel nostalgic and sad, simply take the road or street nearest to your home and walk.*

*Refuse to take a straight line. Roam. Take different directions.*

*In no time you will soon feel so much better.*

*Most good doctors will tell you: Walk, it's good for you health, for your back, your legs, your heart, your lungs, and your veins.*

*To walk is the only sport open to everyone; we don't need a license, a stadium, a special outfit.*

*Walking gives us such joy, and a self- satisfaction that, I believe, should be reimbursed by the health care system. Walking? The only drug to consume with passion.*

Al Goguen,
Victoria.

This letter showed up in my local newspaper, a simple, unsolicited testimonial that in the rhythmic movement of walking we can find stillness and peace.

# 7

# Walking Away From Stress

I sometimes think the word STRESSED is an acronym for Staying Tense Relentlessly Every Single Second Every Day, it's a killing position and I'll tell you why. The human body/mind has only one biological response to stress, which has been part of our species for over a million years. It is called the Fight or Flight Response or Reflex and dates back to a time when virtually all stress was of a physical nature. Stress might come in the form of a saber-toothed tiger, a natural disaster or little hairy men with big clubs, and in every case a decision had to be made; confrontation (fight) or retreat (flight). When stressed, the body readies us to do both, with a chemical cascade that prepares us for action and movement.

As soon as we are aware of a stressor the pituitary gland sets in motion a bio-chemical chain of events, which leads to stimulation of the adrenal glands. Almost instantaneously adrenaline floods into the blood stream triggering a series of responses that turns us into a fighting, running machine.

The major responses include:
(I) Increased blood pressure. To deliver more blood to the muscles.
(II) Increased heart rate. Again to push more blood to the muscles involved in movement.

*No problem is so formidable that you can't walk away from it.*

Charles Schultz

*Walking is our best medicine.*

Hippocrates (460BC – 377BC)

*It is impossible to walk rapidly and be unhappy.*

Howard Murphy, M.D.

(III)   Increased rate of breathing to get in more oxygen for action.
(IV)   Increased blood lipids, which the body can use as fuel.
(V)   Increased blood sugar, another source of quick energy for action.
(VI)   Shutting down of digestion as blood goes away from the gut to be used in the muscles.
(VII)   Eyes become focused on the stressor and whatever we are confronted by is regarded as the enemy.
(VIII)   Increased muscle tension as the major muscles prepare for fight or flight.

This is a wonderful response, which has kept our species alive on this planet for multiple millennia. It is the reflex that enables little old ladies to suddenly have the strength to lift a Volkswagen off someone pinned beneath a car wreck. But it's also the reflex which is now killing us, because it is useless in a world where stress comes in the form of gridlock on the roads, noisy children, bills which you can't pay, in-laws or bosses who don't like your style and many other stressors that cannot be satisfactorily dealt with by fighting or running screaming out of the building.

Mark Twain said that, *To a hammer, all problems look like nails* and to the human body/mind every stressor looks like a fight or flight situation. It's also important to realize that the body doesn't know the difference between an actual stressful situation and a well-imagined disaster or problem that might happen in the future. Again, the wisdom of Mark Twain is appropriate, *In my life I've experienced many terrible things, one or two of which actually happened.*

So you get the picture. We have only **one** biological response to stress or perceived stress (which is all the same) and that response **prepares us for physical action**. (Fight or Flight)

If you're stressed on a daily basis and do nothing to resolve the stress, it begins to take up residence in your body. Blood pressure creeps up, digestion begins to falter, the heart beats faster, blood sugar becomes more unstable and muscles (particularly neck and back) start to contract and ache. Fortunately nature provides us with a simple solution, which I often think of as the three 'A's (Activity Absorbs Anxiety). When you are stressed, upset, tense or angry, you are often able to change your mood by something as simple as taking a walk. When I was a professor and had a difficult and stressful day, if I drove home, I'd drive my stress and tension

*Above all, do not lose your desire to walk.
Every day I walk myself into a state of
well-being and walk away from every illness.*

Soren Kierkegaard

*A fact bobbed up from my memory, that the
ancient Egyptians prescribed walking through a
garden as a cure for mental disorders. It was a
mind-altering drug we took daily.*

Paul Fleischman, *Seedfolks*

home with me, but if I walked home, the problems, which seemed so big in the office, diminished as I walked. (Remember, activity absorbs anxiety). The reason is obvious, the fight or flight reflex prepares the body for action and if you are able to walk, jog, dance and be physically active you deliver to the body what it's programmed to do, and in doing so you calm the hormonal storm within. As a way of treating stress disorders walking has proved at least as effective as medication. In its own way, the rhythm and repetition of walking can also make it a form of active meditation. It sounds too simple, but one of the reasons we struggle with stress is that we have complicated our lives and look for complex solutions when simple ones will suffice. One type of walking, which is specifically designed for stress reduction and peace of mind, is Labyrinth walking, which is described in Chapter 13, *Walking with a Difference*. Paul Dudley White, who was founder of the American Heart Association and President Eisenhower's personal physician, as I noted on page 28, said, *A five mile walk will do more good for an unhappy, but otherwise healthy, adult than all the medicine and psychology in the world.*

Without delving too deeply into the biochemistry of long term stress and depression it is worth noting another reason why physical activity is so important in helping us feel relaxed and positive. Stress and depression (which are often linked) are both associated with lowered levels of dopamine and serotonin in the brain. In a survey of the medical research in this area by Dr. F Chaouloff it is noted that, *A review of the literature on the relationship of exercise to mental health strongly suggests the two are closely linked.* Included in the review are the effects of physical activity in elevating brain dopamine and serotonin.

Writing in Public Health and Nutrition, Dr. J R Fox writes, *In the last 15 years there has been increasing research into the role of exercise a) in the treatment of mental health, and b) in improving mental well-being. There are now several hundred studies and meta-analytic reviews of research in this field.* This body of research suggests that **moderate** regular exercise should be considered as a viable means of treating depression and anxiety and improving mental well-being in the general public.

The effectiveness of walking is now used by a small, but increasing number, of psychotherapists and counselors who, instead of using the

*I have two doctors,
my left leg and my right.*

G M Trevelyan

traditional couch or chair, walk and talk with their clients in a more natural setting. The client gets a two-fold benefit, the biochemical benefits of the walk along with the wisdom of their therapist.

I'm not suggesting walking is the only answer you'll need to deal with stress, but it's a good one. Obviously your mind-set is important, as is your ability to laugh and love and connect with friends. (Note: If you feel some of your *friends* leave you feeling stressed, it might be time to weed your social garden.) Enjoying a healthy diet can be another part of building up stress resiliency, and finding a cause to support also has a way of putting your own problems in perspective.

There are many paths to dealing with stress and it's a good idea to find a path you can walk down.

*It is no measure of health to be well adjusted in a sick society.*

Krishnamurti

*'Twas a dangerous cliff, as they freely confessed,*
*Though to walk near its crest was so pleasant;*
*But over its terrible edge there had slipped*
*A duke and full many a peasant.*
*The people said something would have to be done,*
*But their projects did not at all tally;*
*Some said, "Put a fence 'round the edge of the*
*cliff,"*
*Some, "An ambulance down in the valley."*

First stanza of *A Fence or an Ambulance*
Joseph Malins (1895)
- a poem about prevention -

# 8

# Workplace Walking

Walking is good for your mind, your muscles, your cardio-vascular fitness, your stress levels and your life. Fit employees are absent less often, are more productive, have fewer industrial accidents, make fewer mistakes and cost any company health plan less money than their unfit colleagues. Given the above facts it is clearly in the interest of individual employees to build walking into their working day, and it is also in the interest of employers to support any walking initiatives.

All business organizations have to be aware of the ROI (Return On Investment) of any initiative. The commonly accepted figure for a successful company wellness program is that it will return 3 dollars for every one dollar invested. A well-structured walking program can exceed that ratio many fold because it requires no capital outlay, other than the purchase of pedometers (which are often supplied on a cost recovery basis). The physical, psychological and social benefits of regular walking inevitably have a positive impact on an organization's bottom line. The positive impact of walking goes beyond an ROI and delivers an ROL (Return On Life).

*We could save billions in Healthcare costs if we could just get Americans (and Canadians) on their feet.*

Blue Cross/Blue Shield Association

*Wellness is the last viable long-term cost control strategy.*

University of Michigan
*Worksite Wellness Cost
Benefit Analysis Report*
1979-2004

### The Insurance Industry and Walking

I'm choosing to feature the insurance industry as it is driven by numbers and bottom line benefits. Actuarial figures tell insurance companies all they need to know about the connections between things like smoking and cancer, high blood pressure and heart disease and stroke, and obesity and diabetes (*diabesity*). They also know that as their clients move towards a wellness lifestyle, their medical costs and their insurance claims are reduced.

The following graph comes from *Worksite Wellness* Cost Benefit and Analysis Report 2004. This report was conducted by the University of Michigan and involved over 2 million employees. The graph shows the linear relationship between employees' scores on a Health Risk Appraisal and their annual medical costs. To any insurance agent or employer, the benefits and cost savings of having a healthy work force show up with startling clarity. A 30-point difference on the wellness score made a $1400 difference in the average annual medical costs for each employee. Every positive lifestyle change, such as walking, added points to the wellness score and each single point averaged a $56 saving in medical costs per employee per year.

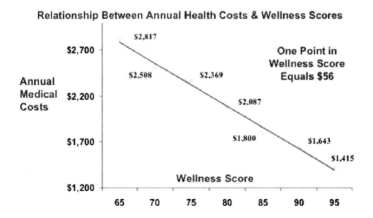

*Better to run (or walk) in fields for health*
*unbought*
*Than fee the doctor for a nauseous draught*
*The wize for care on exercise depend*
*God never made his work for man to mend.*

John Dryden

*Messiah's pointing to the door but*
*no one has the guts to leave the temple.*

Pete Townshend

*As there are people who mend torn garments, so*
*there are physicians who heal the sick; but your*
*duty is far nobler and one befitting a great person*
*— namely to keep people in health.*

Xenophon (400 BC)

I'm not suggesting that you start to increase your walking just to save money, but I am pointing out that walking delivers phenomenal returns for a modest amount of time and effort, which is why we find many insurance companies in the vanguard of walking-based programs. CIGNA use the slogan *Just walk 10,000 steps a day*, Blue Cross/Blue Shield have been distributing pedometers for over 10 years now feature a walking program called *Walking Works*, which you can find at www.walkingworks.com. Other major insurance companies including Aetna, Anthem and Manulife have all supported pedometer-based walking programs. I have personally addressed many insurance groups on the benefits **to them and their clients**, of walking and other activity programs and have found them very receptive and particularly interested in pedometers. When I spoke to Clarica/Sun Life I was delighted that every delegate was given a pedometer bearing the Clarica logo.

Before looking at other work-based programs it's fascinating to look at the origins of research into walking and occupational health.

### Dr. Jerry Morris' Ground-Breaking Studies in Walking

The legendary researcher and physician, Jerry Morris, MD, was probably the first major figure to quantify the benefits of workplace walking. Long before the *Obesity Epidemic* was front-page news, there was concern in Europe and North America about the steady growth in coronary heart disease. Dr. Morris believed that moderate exercise, like regular walking, had a protective effect on the heart and, to the scorn of many of his colleagues, he set out to study it. Firstly, he compared the incidence of heart disease between London bus conductors, who spent all day walking back and forth and up and down the stairs of London's double-decker buses collecting fares, with the bus drivers who sat in the driver's cab and did no walking on the job. The conductors had a third fewer heart attacks than the drivers and in the event that they did experience a heart attack they were much more likely to recover. The drivers were twice as likely to die of a heart attack as the conductors. Dr. Morris found similar results when he compared the active mailmen (letter carriers) to the sedentary mail sorters and telephonists. A separate study looked at how far civil servants walked each day as a part of their commute to work. The further they walked, the less likely they were to experience a heart attack and the lower their blood pressure and blood lipids. Walking

**Presentation to the 1999 Olympic Academy**

By DiNubile and Sherman

The findings are based on a survey of worksite exercise and wellness programs.

- Decreased health care costs
- Decreased absenteeism
- Decreased injury rates
- Decreased employee turnover
- Improved job performance

Cost benefits:
- For exercise-only programs, benefits to the organization were $2.50 for every $1 invested.
- For exercise combined with a comprehensive wellness program, the benefits were $3.50 for every $1 invested.

Similar cost-benefit ratios are still widely reported in both Canada and the USA.

*Out of intense complexities,*
*intense simplicities emerge.*

Winston Churchill

works at work, or on the way to and from work.

Since the pioneering work of Morris there have been hundreds of occupational health studies, which show the protective and health-giving effects of regular physical activity as part of the job. As work has become more sedentary thousands of companies have responded by including physical activity as a part of worksite wellness and by encouraging employees to increase their walking and daily step count.

For years, workplaces have been designed for maximum convenience, but many have become so convenient that employees can go through a whole working day walking only a few steps and burning a handful of calories. But too much convenience kills and some new facilities are being constructed with an eye to giving employees little alternative but to use their legs. The new Sprint world headquarters in Kansas looks more like a college campus. There are no cars inside the road that rings the headquarters, forcing employees to park in the garages outside the ring and walk maybe half a mile to their building. The staircases are wide, airy and feature artwork and big windows whereas the elevators are hydraulic, slow and relatively unattractive. (Think how different this is from any hotel you've ever stayed in). The dining facilities are not necessarily in the most convenient locations, meaning everybody has to walk to lunch. Initially Sprint provided trolleys for those who didn't want to walk, and brollies (umbrellas) for rainy days, but the trolleys were so little used that they have been discontinued. What Sprint has created is a walker-friendly workplace, much in the way that some new communities are being designed to make walking a natural, pleasant and easier way to get about than using a car. One such community in Vancouver, British Columbia is called UniverCity, which, although not completely car-less, has been designed and created with pedestrians and cyclists very much in mind. (See article in online newsletter, *Well,* Summer 2004 http://www.speakwell.com/well/2004summer/iped.php)

In a different attempt to create a walking culture, the Mazda Motor Corporation in Japan pays 1,500 yen a month to any employee who walks a minimum of 4 kilometers (2.5 miles) on their two-way commute, at least 15 times a month. This means that many employees get off the bus or train early so they can qualify for the monthly bonus. Another way in which

*The important thing is this: To be able at any moment to sacrifice what we are for what we could become.*

Charles du Bois

*What we need is not what's new, but what's best.*

Unknown

companies encourage active commuting is to offer a parking 'cash-out', in which an employee may give up an employer-paid parking space in exchange for the value of that space.

A problem faced by many major corporations has been that they have developed excellent workplace fitness and activity programs at company headquarters but are unable to service the majority of their workforce who are spread across the country, and sometimes the planet, at multiple locations. A typical example would be the banking industry where a number of major banks have gymnasia and sports facilities at head office but offer nothing to the thousands of employees at banking branches.

To deal with this problem, my own company joined forces with Telus to structure a walking program, which would be accessible to **all** the 29,000 employees. We created a dedicated portal for Telus employees into the 18,000 km (11,250 mile) virtual walk, Circle Canada. Each employee is being offered a pedometer and can record their daily steps on a database both as an individual and/or part of a team. It is worth mentioning here that programs like this **will not work unless employees use reliable pedometers**. I've watched more than one program implode when participants realized the "steps" showing up on their pedometer had little relation to the actual steps they took.

For further information on Circle Canada and Route 66 see Chapter 5 on Virtual Walking. A company-wide walking program enables **all** employees to participate and enables the company to benefit from a healthier, more productive workforce.

### Small Businesses and Employee Groups

The flexibility and adaptability of workplace walking programs means that they can be used by any small business just as effectively as they can by national and global companies. My own office is testament to that fact, where two people have combined their steps to walk the 18,000k (11,250m) around Canada. We have supplied pedometers to such groups as Tires Unlimited, Cornell University, SaskEnergy, nursing home staff, government departments, retail outlets and garden centers. The fact that walking-based programs have minimal start-up costs, can be self-administered and are not facility based make them an ideal vehicle for

*If it weren't for the rocks in its bed, the stream would have no song.*

Carl Perkins

*As a speaker I regularly pass through Vancouver Airport, which runs a successful incentive based exercise program for employees. After the introduction of the program, days lost to WCB injuries fell from 223 in 1999 to 24 in 2002.*

health promotion for small employee groups.

### Summary: Some ways in which a workplace can become a walk place

1. Create a company policy or mission statement, which supports walking.
2. Make quality pedometers available at low cost or no cost to employees.
3. Establish step-counting goals, such as 10,000 steps per day; one million steps a week for an office group; virtual walking programs such as Circle Canada or Route 66, where participants record steps on a central data base.
4. If buildings have stairways, make them attractive with good lighting, music, attractive décor, artwork and posters reminding everyone of the value of climbing stairs. (Jeff Bezos CEO of Amazon is a great role model to his employees by using the stairs at every opportunity.)
5. Where appropriate, encourage administrators to have some walking meetings.
6. One of the few capital expenditures, which supports all workplace activity programs, including walking, are changing rooms with showers, lockers, hair dryers and mirrors, so that people who walk or cycle to work can return to their workstation feeling and looking good.
7. While it doesn't directly link to walking, health screening can be a major catalyst for employees to make positive lifestyle changes. People with elevated blood pressure, weight problems or unhealthy lipid profiles can be made aware of the benefits of walking and the availability of company walking programs.
8. Plato noted that, *It was a sick place where one had to be a fool or a martyr to do the right (healthy) thing.* Create a workplace where physical activity is supported; where, if possible, there is some flexibility during the workday allowing employees time for a walk, and where 'doing the right (healthy) thing' is facilitated and supported.
9. There is no more natural and practical way to be active than taking a daily, life-saving walk and any program, scheduling or facility design, which supports this, supports everybody in the organization.

*Truth comes knocking on the door, and you say,*
Go away!! I'm looking for the truth.

Robert M. Pirsig

---

*Nearly all advances in medical treatment lead to increasing cost of health care. Only wellness leads to improvement of general health status with a modest investment and impressive cost benefit ratio.*

University of Michigan

Health Management Resource Center

2004 Survey of over 2 million employees.

---

*If you win the rat race, you're still a rat.*

Unknown

10. By extending the company walking program to clients and customers there is a tremendous opportunity to have customers identify with your company and thus create customer loyalty. When both employees and clients are involved in a common program, it provides a natural company/client interface between customer and company.

This book is published by a progressive company, Trafford Publishing. Trafford is a non-traditional, on-demand publisher, which filled my needs both practically and professionally. One of the things I like about Trafford is the wellness philosophy, which is part of the DNA of the company. Bus passes are provided to employees to encourage them to leave their cars at home. Cycle storage is planned. Their medical plan is extensive and embraces alternative medicine and prevention, in addition to traditional allopathic medicine. They will pay for nicotine patches for smokers and cover acupuncture and massage where appropriate.

On a more global level, they are passionate recyclers, try to use alternative energy sources and have pledged 1.6 million dollars to help publish and save endangered languages. It's the sort of company we feel comfortable dealing with.

*A good education turns a child into an adult without losing or removing the child. Too many adults are dead children who have lost their ability to play.*

Martin Collis

*Man made the school, God made the schoolyard.*

Walter Bagehot

*All life should be lived as play.*

Plato

# 9

# Where Do The Children Play?

This chapter addresses much more than the use of pedometers and walking programs in schools. It provides an overview of the multiple factors that make it too easy for children to fall far short of their potential as young, active human beings.

One of the best things that ever happened to 17-year-old Drew Garland was being barred from his school bus after a conflict with another student. It forced him out of a sedentary lifestyle and into a walking routine that helped him drop more than 100 pounds. He freefell to 235 pounds from 340 in one year.

*I had lost a little bit before that,* the DeKalb High School junior said, *but when I started walking everywhere, that's when I started losing way more. I wouldn't sit around the house and eat as much.*

His mother, Christine, also said he quit eating whole bags of potato chips and boxes of crackers at one sitting. He had never thought of it this way, but having to walk to or from school 2 1/2 miles away, in addition to hoofing it as simple transportation around town, was taking him back toward what his body was built for: a daily workout that still would have been an easy day for his genetic ancestors, the hunter-gatherers.

*Any town that doesn't have sidewalks doesn't love its children.*

Margaret Mead

*We cannot always build the future for our youth, but we can build our youth for the future.*

Franklin D. Roosevelt

Being barred from the school bus probably saved Drew Garland's young life and certainly increased the likelihood that his life would be longer and healthier.

### The Bad News

There is bad news and some good news about the fitness and fatness of our children. The bad news is very, very bad, and the good news is that we're just beginning to realize how bad and put programs in place to help reverse the insanity of poorly fed and under-exercised children in the wealthiest nations on the planet. People tend not to change when they see the light, but are more likely to do so when they feel the heat and finally, after 25 years of statistics showing increasing numbers of fat, unfit children, we are feeling enough heat to initiate change. The following summary will show why changes are vital.

Year by year, from the sandbox to the seniors in high school, our children have been getting fatter and fatter. We are breeding a generation who will die before their parents in increasing numbers. We are killing our children with kindness, which comes disguised as convenience. Children have been immunized against every disease except inactivity. In the late 60s, Crosby, Stills, Nash and Young commanded us to, *Teach your children well* and we haven't.

Our culture has created a perfect storm for children to be fat and inactive, by making high calorie/low nutrient food available at every turn and by removing the need for calorie burning activity from their lives. When conservative government agencies report on childhood obesity the word *epidemic* is frequently used. The reasons are very, very easy to document.

- The average child will be in school for 11,000 hours by the time they graduate. During this time they will watch 15,000 hours of TV. They will have had 750 hours of physical education, if they're lucky.
- The advent of computers, Game Boys, X-Boxes, Sony Play Stations and multi-function cell phones mean thousands more sedentary hours in front of a screen.
- In 1989, 15% of US homes had computers; in 2006 that figure is now over 84%.

Ralph Nader responds to a question about the dangers of commercialization:

*Q: You've blasted corporate America for "commercializing everything it touches". What strikes you as the most obscene example of commercialization?*

*A: The commercialization of childhood is truly the most offensive. Basically, corporations have decided that kids under 12 are a lucrative market, and they sell directly to them, subverting parental authority. The idea is to reach these millions of kids who are in a vulnerable, impressionable state, even starting at 2, 3, 4 years old, to get them to nag their parents to buy the products. What are they selling these kids? Bad diets, fat and sugar, teaching them to be addicts. They are addicting them to watching 30, 40 hours of screens – video, television, computer screens. The commercialization of children is a pervasive form of electronic child molestation.*

- The food industry in North America spends over **35 billion** dollars on advertising, overwhelming the few million that health related organizations can generate to promote healthy eating.
- By the time a North American child leaves school, most will have been exposed to at least 100,000 expensive, persuasive and slickly produced commercials for junk foods and soft drinks. Not surprisingly a number of European countries have banned such commercials from TV programs aimed at children under the age of 12. The only state or province to do this in North America is Quebec, reflecting a more European approach to protecting young children from indoctrination by multi-national food and drink vendors.
- 85% of North American homes have a microwave.
- Across North America in the 1990s and spilling into the 21$^{st}$ century school physical education has been reduced and in some cases removed.
- For reasons of safety, convenience and necessity, an increasing number of children are transported to and from school in cars and buses. (They are powered by hydrocarbons rather than carbohydrates.)
- In the past 40 years, the size of many fast food servings has increased 4 fold.
  - The one–ounce hamburger patty has become a 1/4 pounder and more.
  - The 6 or 8–ounce soft drink has become a 32-ounce Big Gulp.
  - The medium popcorn has gone from 3 cups to 16 cups.
- Children, on average, spend 40% of their disposable income on *convenience* food and if they eat *Biggie* fries, *Whoppers* and *Supersized* portions, many will become *biggie, whopping, supersized* kids.
- 20% of 1- and 2-year-olds in North America drink pop.
- With increasing numbers of single parent families, and families in which both parents work, children are likely to eat packaged foods and fast foods, and indulge in unsupervised TV watching.

This is not an anti-technology rant; TVs, computers and microwaves are not going to go away, nor would I want them to. Our need is for children to be able to live well in a culture that makes it easy for them to live badly.

### Run Johnny Run

Music and Lyrics by Martin Collis

*I'll sing you the song about Johnny Spain, I'll start when he's 6 years old.*
*His daddy worked in a pulp mill, that's what I've been told.*
*His mummy she worked in a baker's shop, she was a waitress on the sly*
*And Johnny did the best he could with the things their cash could buy.*
*Run Johnny run. Your life has just begun.*
*One bright September morning Johnny started out to school*
*He wasn't good at reading and some kids called him a fool*
*But once a week for a special treat the kids went to the gym*
*And Johnny knew without being told it was the place for him*
*Run Johnny run. Now you'll have some fun.*

*He should have had fun every week but it didn't work out that way*
*They closed the gym for 20 days rehearsing for a play.*
*They used it for the school bazaar and to let the people vote.*
*And it seemed to him the beautiful gym was getting ever more remote.*
*Run Johnny run. You gotta chase your fun.*
*His mum and dad weren't home that much so Johnny had a key*
*He could open the fridge and the house and to turn on the T.V.*
*He got junk food for his body he had T.V. on his mind*
*And the tiny figures on the T.V. Screen were the best friends he could find.*
*Run Johnny run. You're a son of a gun.*

*Along with Friends and Family Guy Johnny watched a lot of sports*
*And every day a different play would occupy his thoughts*
*But basketball above them all set his eyes and mind agleam*
*So he walked down to the gas station and signed up for a team.*
*Run Johnny run. You can run and gun.*
*He bought himself some Converse shoes and his very own basketball.*
*They held a lot of practices but Johnny made them all.*
*But when it came to making cuts and 6 kids had to go*
*One of them was Johnny Spain who was short and fat and slow.*
*Run Johnny run. You're not the chosen one.*

Continued on page 170

We have to be able to reverse trends like those documented by Lyle and colleagues in the American Journal of Health Promotion.

|  | Grade | | |
| --- | --- | --- | --- |
|  | 3$^{rd}$ | 5$^{th}$ | 8$^{th}$ |
| Ate breakfast | 98.6 | 94.4 | 85.2% |
| Ate fruit | 64.6 | 55.9 | 37.1% |
| Ate vegetables | 56.1 | 49.5 | 41.6% |
| Drank fruit juice | 44.0 | 47.4 | 32.0% |
| Drank soft drinks | 21.4 | 30.8 | 57.1% |

The patterns are obvious – there is a gradual decline in eating breakfast and a marked decline in the consumption of fruits, vegetables and juices, and there is a big jump in the intake of soft drinks, which more than doubled between grades 3 and 8. Little exercise and lots of soft drinks can lead to soft kids. Children that consume large numbers of calories need more and more physical activity and they're getting less and less.

### Convenience Kills

In the story of the Pied Piper, the parents panicked when the Piper came for the children. Now the Pied Piper of convenience and commerce lures children towards a lifestyle that will decrease their personal potential and steal years from their lives. We've gone from Generation X to Generation XXL and our craving for convenience is a major reason why.

- Daily physical education is not convenient in schools. You need special facilities, equipment, showers, organization, well–trained teachers and safety precautions. It is much more convenient for administrators to decrease or eliminate physical education. The rationale is often that parents are asking for more academic content, but this doesn't bare close scrutiny. I would challenge any educator to show me statistics that when a school goes to quality daily physical education that academic scores go down, in fact the reverse is usually true, academic performance goes up. In 2001, the Center for Disease Control in the USA noted: *Nationwide only 56.1% of students were enrolled in a physical education class. Nationwide 29.1% of students attended a high school physical education class daily, down*

### Run Johnny Run (cont'd)

*Aboard the education train he got to junior high*
*But he was a different Johnny Spain - he was growing up kind of sly*
*He wouldn't do cross-country, he had problems with his knees*
*And every week old Johnny the freak would develop a new disease.*
*Run Johnny run. Your downward slide's begun.*
*Just look in any beer-hall and it's full of Johnny Spains*
*They're bored with life at 25 and an awful lot remains*
*But I look at them quite guiltily for I know without a doubt*
*There's a jock inside each Johnny Spain that never could get out.*
*Run Johnny run. Run for your life!*

### Get Real

A 2006 survey commissioned by the Canadian Medical Association showed that 9% of Canadian parents believed their children were overweight. In reality, 26% of Canadian kids are overweight or obese according to data collected by Statistics Canada.

*When the student is ready,*
*the teacher will appear.*

Rumi

*from 42% in 1991.* The International Life Sciences Institute found that *Fewer than one in four children get 20 minutes of vigorous physical activity every day. Also, less than one in four reported getting at least a 1/2 hour of any type of physical activity every day.*

- Cars and buses are a convenient way to get children to school. There are concerns about bicycle safety and storage—the children are *safe* in their glass, metal and plastic containers and everybody can have a few extra few minutes in bed. But the convenience deprives them of much needed movement and exercise. In response to safety concerns, there is a growing movement called *The Walking School Bus* in which parents chaperone groups of children on their walk to school.

- Convenience stores sell convenience foods that are typically high in sugar, fat and salt. I once wrote a verse about Pringles potato chips:

    *When god created potatoes*
    *And donated them to man*
    *It wasn't to be crushed and fried*
    *And served in a tennis ball can.*

- Typically, packaged cookies and baked goods use the cheapest and most damaging hydrogenated fats. Fruit *drinks* are loaded with sugar in the form of high fructose corn syrup. In one meal at a fast food franchise, in addition to getting lots of bad fat, sugar and salt, a child (or an adult) can consume their complete daily requirement of calories. In order to sell 2 for 1 specials and get bigger and bigger, some pizza chains have to use the cheapest cheese for their toppings and artery clogging fats for their crust.

- TV is the ultimate convenience device. If the kids are acting up, click on the cartoons. Instead of a bedtime story, pop in a Disney video. Unsupervised TV watching leaves children exposed to daily doses of murder, mayhem, sex and slick commercials.

*Society is always taken by surprise
at any new example of common sense.*

R. W. Emerson

My former student and good friend, Gord
Medd, was told in high school, *You'll never amount
to anything.* He is now one of the younger assistant
superintendents in the California school system.
Gord gets up at 5am to go to his fitness club, runs
most days, plays soccer, coaches his two boys and
practices an administrative style that Tom Peters
called M.B.W.A., *Management By Walking About.*

The last words I can remember my traditional
old school principal saying to me were, *Grow up;
get serious and wipe that stupid smile off your face!* I
ignored those three injunctions and now get paid
for the things I used to get beaten for.

A recent piece of research noted that children who watch 1 hour or less TV per day have a 3% chance of becoming obese. Children that watch 3 hours or more per day have a 25% chance of becoming obese.

Children with a TV in their bedroom are far more likely to be overweight and obese than those that don't, and one third of children aged 2 to 7 have bedroom TV's according to the Kaiser Family Foundation.

• Ritalin and similar drugs are a convenient way to 'treat' a hyperactive child, and there is little doubt that they are over prescribed. The Physician's Desk Reference specifically states that Ritalin *should not be used in children under 6 years of age*, but in 1993 US physicians wrote 200,000 prescriptions for Ritalin and similar stimulants for children 5 years old and younger. (Ritalin is a stimulant that has the paradoxical effect of tranquilizing highly active children). In 1995 more than 6 million psychiatric prescriptions were written for American school aged children. (This information comes from the challenging and well–researched book by John Robbins, *Reclaiming Our Health*.) Ritalin is convenient for parents, doctors, teachers and administrators but psychiatrists Barkley and Cunningham, after analyzing 17 studies, noted that Ritalin *does not enhance learning*.

### Solutions

The massive problem of unfit, overweight children will not change with low level tinkering of school programs or by individuals swimming against the cultural tide. The only way we get significant measurable improvement is to gradually change the culture. This is a tall order involving politics, economics, human rights, mass media, the health care systems and education.

However, there are no innocent bystanders and if we are not part of the solution we are part of the problem. Every parent, every politician, every pedagogue and every physician needs to lend their voice and influence to

There is no study that shows that after the introduction of quality daily physical education into a school or district that academic performance went down. There are a number of studies that show academic performance improves when school children are active on a daily basis. In the 2006 Canadian Medical Association Survey 92% of parents support mandatory physical education in K through 12.

*Where does magic come from?*
*I think magic's in the learning.*

Dar Williams

create an environment where physical activity is a vital part of the school and the home experience

DON'T OVERLOOK THIS SECTION. EVEN IF YOU HATE GRAPHS, TAKE THE TIME TO SEE THE POWER AND SIGNIFICANCE OF THE MEANING OF THE 3 BAR GRAPHS FROM THE CALIFORNIA DEPARTMENT OF EDUCATION.

I sometimes ask people the following question:

*What if there was a miracle program or product that could help reverse the epidemic of childhood obesity and had side effects such as enhanced health and self-esteem and **better academic performance**?*

Surely every School Board, teacher and parent would want it featured in every school.

**There is a miracle program; it's called physical activity!!**

A good physical education/physical activity program will result in fitter, slimmer, healthier students and an overall improvement in academic performance.

The California Department of Education administers standardized tests of academic performance known as the Stanford Achievement Tests. In 2001, for the first time they introduced a state mandated 6-item physical fitness test (FitnessGram) for students in grades 5, 7 and 9. Someone in the department got the bright idea of seeing if there was a relationship between students' fitness levels and their academic performance. The results should have made the front page of every newspaper on the Continent. **There was a perfect correlation between students' fitness scores and their performance in math and reading. This study involved nearly one million children and was not requested by physical educators or other special interest group.**

Quite simply the study showed that as fitness improved, so did academic performance in reading and math. The astonishing feature of

*Schools should not be sausage factories where facts and information are stuffed into children. They should be more like oyster farms where you take the oysters and stimulate them, challenge them and even irritate them and every so often produce a pearl.*

M. L. Collis

*It is a miracle that curiosity survives formal education.*

Albert Einstein

*Nobody in the game of football should be called a genius. A genius is someone like Norman Einstein.*

Joe Theisman,
Former quarterback and
current TV analyst.

these data is that for all 3 grades there is not one bar out of alignment. The fittest children score the highest and the least fit achieve the lowest academic scores. As measured fitness levels improve, so does academic performance.

**IF YOU HAVE ANY INTEREST IN CHILDREN LOOK AT THESE GRAPHS.**

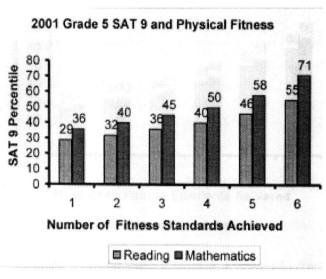

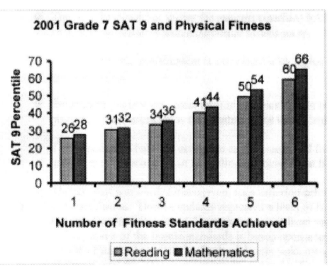

*It is easier to build strong children than to repair broken adults.*

Frederick Douglas

*I don't believe in original sin,
I believe in original splendor.*

George Sheehan

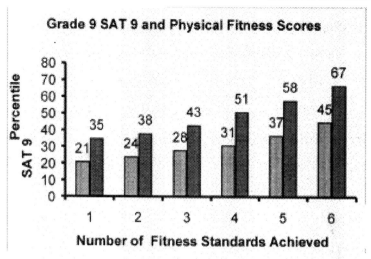

Grade 9 SAT 9 and Physical Fitness Scores

I rest my case. Children are vigorous young animals that do well when they are active and less well when they're sedentary.

### What Can Schools Do?

This book is focused on walking and steps and I'm not proposing that giving every child a pedometer would solve the declining fitness of our children. But pedometers are increasingly being used to make children aware of their activity level; to help them relate calories consumed (particularly junk food calories and pop) to the amount of effort it takes to 'burn-off' those calories. The Circle Canada program developed at Speakwell is being used to teach geography, history and for numerous inter-class competitions, as children have fun visiting every Province and Territory and are motivated to getting more and more steps. A Route 66 will soon be available so that children can experience the famous route from Chicago to LA.

At the end of this chapter I'll give some examples of the creative use of pedometers in schools.

### What Schools Need to do to Help Children be More Physically Active and Lose Some Weight.

1. Children learn skills best when their bodies are young, when it's easy for their nerves and muscles to learn new patterns of movement. This means we need skilled physical education

### Hardly the Breakfast of Champions

In a recent piece of research commissioned by the *Globe and Mail* newspaper and CTV (Published in the *Globe and Mail* Sept. 5, 2006 in an article by Andre Picard), it was shown that many popular children's breakfast cereals contained as much sugar as a chocolate bar. The researchers compared the amount of sugar in a 50g (1.75oz) serving of cereal with that contained in various popular chocolate bars. For example, a bowl of *Post Sugar Crisp* contained more sugar than a *Kit Kat* bar, a *Mr. Big*, a *Snickers* bar and numerous other chocolate treats.

Historically, it's fascinating to trace how popular and healthy cereals from the late 1890's became the big-business sugarcoated staples in the 21st Century. Postum Cereals was founded by C.W. Post in 1895. Their first successful product was *Postum*, which was referred to as a 'cereal beverage'. This was quickly followed by *Grape Nuts*, one of the first cold breakfast cereals. Postum Cereals was soon renamed Post Cereals and quickly began to buy other food and beverage companies and in 1929 became General Foods. General Foods was acquired by Philip Morris Companies in 1985. Three years later, in 1988, Philip Morris paid 13 billion dollars to add Kraft Foods to its empire. Kraft and General Foods were merged and Philip Morris was reborn as the Altria Group to distance itself from the stigma of cigarettes.

What this means is that the corporate group that brings you *Marlboro, Benson & Hedges* and *Virginia Slims* cigarettes, various brands of beer ranging from *Miller* to *Henry Weinhard* also makes your children's breakfast cereal.

. Dietitian Leslie Beck says, "I think parents know that these cereals are sugary, but they don't understand the extent. When you say, *your child is eating the equivalent of a Mars bar for breakfast,* that should hit home."

specialists in kindergarten and throughout elementary school. What young children need is a vocabulary of movement that makes it easy for them to join a team or activity when they become teenagers.

2. Get soft drink machines and junk food dispensers out of schools completely. They can be replaced with healthy alternatives. Also, get rid of any signage or sponsorship from fast food/junk food companies.

3. Every grade from K through 12 needs QUALITY DAILY PHYSICAL EDUCATION. I underline the word 'quality' because poor physical education programs actually turn students off physical activity. It is important to have physical education specialists to teach classes and to assist non-specialists in keeping physical education interesting and relevant.

4. Don't sell junk food to raise funds. The Girl Guides long ago figured out that they could make a lot of money with cookies. At a National PTA Convention in San Antonio the exhibit halls were not dominated by information about supporting academic advancement or student health, but by multi-national confectioners like Mars, Nestle and Hershey. The Sugar Association was there to refute the *myths* that sugar could cause hyperactivity, obesity, diabetes or tooth decay. "If your child loves sweet treats, there's no need to worry", their literature stated.

5. Support all efforts to encourage children to get to school under their own power. Create good cycle storage, support chaperoned walk-to-school groups for younger children and don't spend hundreds of thousands of dollars creating convenient traffic flow patterns so children can be dropped off right at the door from their parents' cars and SUVs. For children who are bused to school it would be a good idea to have the drop off station a 1/2 mile or about 1 kilometer from the schools so that they get a walk at the beginning and end of the school day. On rainy days this could be changed.

6. Use a test like *FitnessGram* (http://www.cooperinst.org/ftgmain.asp) so children and their parents can be aware of the students' fitness and body composition.

*It is not talking, but walking,*
*that will bring us to heaven.*

Matthew Henry

---

**From Generation X to Generation XXL**

Dr. Mark Tremblay, an internationally
renowned researcher on pediatric exercise,
reported that in the 20-year period between 1979-
1998 there was a 160% increase in obesity for
Canadian boys and 192% increase in obesity for
Canadian girls. There has been no indication since
that those trends are slowing down

---

7. Make physical activity high profile, like the school that created SPARC (Student Physical Activity Record Card). This documented the students' growth, development in strength and flexibility, aerobic capacity and body composition and was presented to them along with their graduation certificate.

8. Don't confuse physical education with athletics. Inter school sports are great for the physically gifted and sport loving students, just as a school orchestra is good for young musicians. However, where the coach is also a physical education teacher, physical education sometimes becomes like an extra practice for the elite athletes rather than a stimulating activity experience for all the students.

9. No smoking anywhere on school grounds and this includes teachers and support staff. The more teachers model wellness behaviors the more credibility they will have. What they do shouts so loud that children cannot hear what they say. (The same applies to parents).

10. In order to make an impact on students, physical education needs to be relevant and stimulating. When I was a young teacher I realized that not every child liked traditional physical education, but outside school would pay their own money to do things like yoga, weight training, martial arts and aerobic classes. Check out what's fashionable and, particularly in high school, build it into the curriculum.

## Using Pedometers to Encourage Activity

Activity begins at home. A recent study of children in Halifax, Nova Scotia, found that children averaged 12,000 steps a day on school days, but only 10,000 steps a day on weekends when they were at home!! Parents should make sure their own house is in order before suggesting that schools should be keeping their kids in shape.

For children in the 7 to 11 year old range 10,000 steps is a minimum goal. Active children (and all young children need to be active) should typically be in the 12,000 to 15,000-step range. Children are generally lighter, take smaller steps and have time to play, all of which makes higher step totals realistic. As they become teenagers many children become more sedentary; homework increases, some get jobs, increasing amounts of time

**Class set of Speakwell H215 pedometers**

*Forgive no error you recognize, it will repeat itself, increase, and afterwards our pupils will not forgive us what we forgave.*

Yevtushenko

are spent with cell phones and computers and unstructured active play often decreases. Step totals tend to go down but the need for activity is vital in developing bodies. Again, 10,000 steps should be a minimum goal with 12,000 steps a desirable number.

Remember, children (and most adults) won't do something just because it's good for them, the more steps come from 'fun' activities or walking to a destination such as school, the store or a friend's house the more likely they are to accumulate. A friend of mine who teaches grade 2 in a lower socio-economic area intuitively felt that her students paid more attention and did better work after they were active. In addition to their PE, she would lead her class on a 2k (1 1/4 mile) walk around the school grounds. At first, it was a challenge for some children, but they quickly adjusted and looked forward to their walk. Children who went around quickly were allowed to play on the climbing equipment till the teacher arrived with the main group. Once back in the classroom students' attention level rose and they were ready to learn.

### Pedometers in Schools

In Chapter 4 I discussed the many varieties of pedometers available and in the section *Pick a Practical Pedometer* suggested some of the best buys at different prices. More detail can be found on my website at www.speakwell.com/well/2005autumn/pedometer.php. The main criteria in selecting pedometers for use by children is whether the pedometers are accurate, reliable and robust. In order to assist schools with equipping children with pedometers, my own company, Speakwell, markets boxes of 16 H215 pedometers (our *best buy* in the *less than $20* category) for $249 CAD and $225 USD [Note: these are 2006 prices and might fluctuate.] The sectional boxes are useful for teachers keeping track of the classroom sets.

I will repeat the advice I have given earlier in this book about trying to save money by purchasing cheap pedometers. In my own testing I failed to find a reliable, accurate and robust pedometer that was really inexpensive. All the existing school programs, such as *Circle Canada, Route 66,* one million steps and interclass competitions become meaningless if the children know that the totals on their pedometers don't reflect their actual

## FITNESSGRAM®

If you are a teacher, administrator or parent, consider getting FITNESSGRAM for your school or school district. I've sat in with the FITNESSGRAM Board that is made up of elite pediatric exercise scientists, epidemiologists and experts in test and measurement and who are constantly reviewing and refining the FITNESSGRAM instrument.

The FITNESSGRAM assessment includes items in the following three areas of fitness.

Aerobic Capacity (select one)
- The Pacer – a 20-meter progressive, multi-stage shuttle run set to music (the PACER is also available in a 15-meter distance).
- On Mile Walk/Run
- Walk Test available for secondary students.

Body Composition (select one)
- Percent Body Fat – calculated from triceps and calf skinfold measurements.
- Body Mass Index – calculated from height and weight.

Muscle Strength, Endurance and Flexibility
- Abdominal Strength – Curl-up Test
- Trunk Extensor Strength and Flexibility – Trunk Lift
- Flexibility (select one)
    o Back-saver Sit-and-reach
    o Shoulder Stretch
- Upper Body Strength (select one)
    o 90 degree Push-up
    o Flexed Arm Hang
    o Modified Pull-up

FITNESSGRAM is a health related physical fitness assessment. Each of the test items was selected to assess important aspects of a student's health related fitness, not skill or agility. Students are compared not with each other, but to health fitness standards, carefully established for each age and gender, that indicate good health. More information on the standards is available in the Reference Guide. Once the assessment has been done, the FITNESSGRAM report provides objective, personalized feedback and positive reinforcement which are vital to changing behavior and serve as a communications link between teachers and parents and students. [For more information go to www.fitnessgram.net or www.humankinetics.com]

step count. There are plenty of good pedometers on the market and the better ones will usually provide a help line to troubleshoot any questions you have and, of course, guarantee to immediately replace any pedometer which malfunctions.

### Measuring Stride Length

(I)   Wet Walk. After wetting the soles of shoes walk at a regular pace on a dry surface such as asphalt or concrete. Step length is measured from the back of one heel to the back of the other heel.

(II)   The same result can be obtained indoors using gymnastic chalk on the soles of shoes or feet and once again measuring from heel to heel.

(III)   Take a standard distance and count the number of steps.

400-meter track. Walk one lap and count the number of steps you take. Divide the number of steps into 400 e.g. 400 ÷ 492 = .81 meter stride length. For a 440-yard track use the same procedure to get stride in inches.

Other standard distances might be a 100 yard or 100 meter track; a regulation US football field, which is 100 yards; the distance from the goal line to the top of the penalty area in a soccer field, which is 18 yards; on a rugby field there is a 22 meter line.

Once you have an average step length it's easy to calculate distance walked by multiplying step length by the number of steps.

### Activities

#### A. Counting Calories

This can be done in association with a math, science or home economics class.

1.   Record Body Weight. In the US this will be in pounds and in Canada in kilograms.

2.   If the body weight is in pounds, convert it to kilograms by multiplying by 0.45.

3.   If you are walking at a steady pace (somewhere around 3 mph or 4.8 to 5kph) you can calculate the number of calories you burn per minute.

4.   Multiply your bodyweight in kg by 0.08.

## Just A Teacher

By Martin Collis

*What do you know, it's Harold
Brown.
It's been a long old time.
The way old buddies drift apart
It surely is a crime.
So what about those kids of yours?
I bet they've long since grown.
They were the best, but since they've
left the nest
How far have they flown?*

*My daughter she's a lawyer,
And she works in real estate.
She lives down in Los Angeles
And business is going great.
My older boy he's a doctor
And here's a funny twist.
He always was a shy one
Now he's a gynaecologist.*

*But what about the youngest one
The brightest of the three?
I always felt that he'd succeed
In what he chose to be.
How come you haven't mentioned
him?
Are you holding out on me?
I really felt that Tommy Brown
Would climb the highest tree.*

*Oh Tommy; he's just a teacher
In a small Alberta town.
For every triple feature
You get someone who plays the clown.
He was offered success on a silvery
plate
And he went and stared it down.
He just took a job and followed his
fate
To a small Alberta town.*

*So your daughter works in real estate
Selling condos to the rich.
And your doctor son he's a real wiz
At fixing that terrible itch.
And Tommy's found a little town
To make himself a niche.
You ask me who's successful?
Well, I can tell you which.*

*For my grand son had a handicap
And it made him insecure.
And no special ed. psychologist
Could offer him a cure.
But then he got a teacher
By the name of Tommy Brown
Who got through to my grandson
And he turned his life around."*

*So that's the way I heard about
Your unsuccessful one.
Helping out my grandson
Is not the only thing he's done.
He has a special way with kids
And of making learning fun.
When thirty children leave his class
They each feel number one!*

*So, Tommy, he's just a teacher
In a small Alberta Town.
It's him and it's teachers like him
That make the world go round.
He's got a pick-up truck and a trailer
For a couple of thousand down.
He's got the love of everybody
In that small Alberta town.*

This song is based on a true story told to me by a young teacher in the town of Medicine Hat, Alberta. I often use it when I speak with teachers. It is recorded on my CD Beaten Tracks and can be ordered from www.speakwell.com/wellMart/index.shtml.

5.  In one minute of walking someone weighing 100 lbs (45 kg)
    would burn:

    Bodyweight 45 x 0.08 = 3.6 calories

Once you establish a calories-per-minute rate you can have some fun.

(I)   How many calories would you burn if you walked for 1/2 hour?

(II)  If there are 220 calories in a chocolate bar, how long would it take
      to burn them off by walking?

(III) Guess how many steps you would have to walk and how long it
      would take to 'walk-off' a McDonalds Big Mac (570 cals), large fries
      (540 cals) and a chocolate shake (580 cals)? Total for the meal: 1710
      cals.

If we have our 100 lb student who burns 3.6 calories a minute walking at
about 3mph (4.8 kph) you can calculate that it would take **about 8 hours to
walk off your McDonalds meal**!! Something you never hear at the Golden
Arches is *Let's have a Big Mac and all the trimmings and then do an 8 hour walk.*

### Random Step Number Draw

Have a couple of prizes (parents and local merchants will usually help) for a
given weekly step total. The number will be random, but it will be above a
designated minimum. For this activity each child will need their own
pedometer.

You can also have a prize to guess how many steps the teacher has done in
one day or one week. Students can then calculate how far he/she has walked
and how many calories he/she has burned.

### Walking Away the Calories

This can be done with or without pedometers. On a regular basis, maybe
as part of a PE class, or maybe just to get the children outside, pick one
food item and have students guess how far to walk to *walk off* the calories.
With elementary children 25 steps per calorie is near enough, or if you just
want to do distance, 17 1/2 yards per calorie or 16 meters per calorie are
reasonable approximations. The idea is to give students a feeling for how
far you have to walk to *burn off* a Coke, chocolate bar, shake, or any other
food or drink with which kids will be familiar.

*At the end of the twentieth century many students were trying to find themselves. In the twenty first century many students have a better idea, they are going out to make themselves.*

Unknown

Route 66 PED at www.speakwell.com

**Your First Million**

The million step chart is shown on page 59 in Chapter 4 *Getting to 10,000*. Kids love numbers, particularly big ones like a million, and they will have a lot of fun and interest marking off 10,000 step increments until the figure of one million is reached. This total is easily reached by a class of 20 to 25 children, but can also be accomplished by individuals.

**Circle Canada**

This is proving to be a huge success in schools as it integrates geography, history and social studies with a cumulative walking program. Starting in Victoria, a class of students can combine their steps on a walking tour of Canada. At each major city along the route there is a pop-up with insider information about where to eat, which trails to hike or ski, local jokes, famous residents and festivals in addition to historical background. A class of 25 students recording their steps each day should be able to get around the 18,000 kilometers in 3 to 4 months. Even if everyone doesn't have a pedometer it's easy to convert kilometers or miles into steps so that every student contributes. To help people around we have provided a few surprise bonus rides, somewhat like snakes and ladders, but there are no snakes. Once through Edmonton walkers are picked up by a CN train and whisked to Saskatoon, and later on there are boat trips and other forms of transportation to reward people for walking so far. (See Chapter 5 *Virtual Walking*)

Steps can be recorded at the Speakwell website (www.speakwell.com) by clicking on the *PED Circle Canada* button. Students can record their steps on PED and get a personal step total in addition to having their steps go to a designated group total. Progress is measured by a red line that passes through every province and territory in Canada. Under development at the time of writing is *PEDal* for cyclists and a Route 66 walking program for those who want to tour the USA.

At the Academy of the Sierras, which bills itself as the world's first therapeutic boarding school for overweight adolescents, every student wears a pedometer. With mandatory pre-breakfast walks and other physical activities the students have no problem recording over 10,000 steps per day. The pedometer is used, along with a lot of behavior modification and therapy, to help students understand that they have been living a lifestyle that is incompatible with health and enjoyment and that

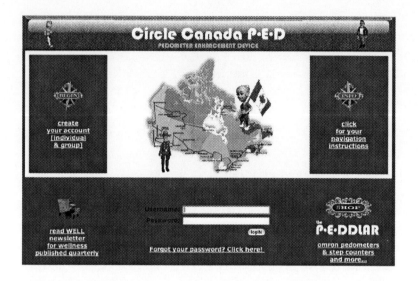

Circle Canada PED at www.speakwell.com

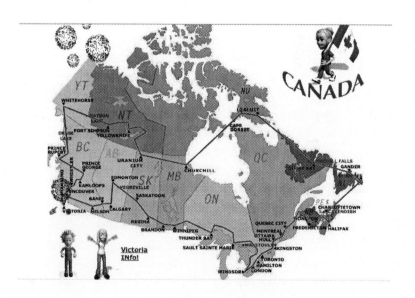

movement is one of the keys to reclaim their youth.

## Summary

Any creative way we can find to get children moving is positive. Pedometers are important motivational and educational tools, which are affordable and can be used in many parts of the curriculum. However, a pedometer alone might not have a big impact on activity behaviors. The big positive changes come when pedometers are linked with programs, education and, of course, inspirational teaching.

*If you want to forget your troubles, wear shoes that are too tight.*

The Houghton Line

*It must be the shoes.*

Spike Lee

# 10

# Walking Shoes

Some readers might feel this chapter is unnecessary. Isn't walking the activity you can do in any outfit, any time and any place? Isn't the convenience and lack of need for special equipment the reason walking is the single most popular physical activity? The answer to all the above questions is 'yes'. So if you are one of those people who walks daily, loves their shoes and sees no reason to change, maybe this chapter isn't for you. However, we live in an era of specialization and every activity comes with a variety of equipment and accessories. Walking is no exception. Special walking shoes may not be necessities, but they can make a good thing better. Twenty years ago there was no *walking shoe* section in stores selling sporting goods. You'd find some hiking boots, but nothing designed for the regular urban walker. Walking existed a long time before *walking shoes;* in fact walking existed a long time before shoes. A few thousand years ago people probably ridiculed the introduction of sandals, which originally had soles made of sagebrush bark with leather straps to hold them in place. One can imagine parents saying, *All your mother and I needed was our bare feet, now you feel you need those fancy sandals like your friends.* But sandals were here to stay and the Greeks and Romans improved their design and gave us some vocabulary, which is still around today. The word *sandal* comes from the Greek *sandalion* meaning *board*, so the original sandals may have been none too flexible. Roman soldiers often averaged over 20 miles a day

*One who limps is still walking.*

Stanislaw J. Lec

*Make your feet your friends.*

J. M. Barrie

marching in their sandals and our word *mile* is derived from the Latin *milia passum* meaning *1000 double steps*. So two thousand years later it's not surprising that there are still approximately 2000 steps per mile, because that's what *mile* means.

Charles Dickens, wearing leather shoes, often walked up to 20 miles a day and numerous other wanderers have traveled prodigious distances on foot before the existence of Reebok, Rockport and Rykå.

> Between 1953 and 1981 Peace Pilgrim walked more than 25,000 miles back and forth across the States wearing simple canvas sneakers, vowing to *remain a wanderer until mankind has learned the way of peace.*

So you don't have to wait until you buy a pair of designated walking shoes before starting on your 10,000-step program. It can just become another excuse for not starting. *I'll begin when I can afford some proper walking shoes.*

However, in the past few years we've learned a lot about foot mechanics, which you can use to your advantage by getting the right sort of walking shoes for your foot type and the way you walk. Walking shoes have now been designed to not only feel good, but look good, unlike the originals, which looked like nurses' shoes or the dreaded orthopedic shoes.

### Shopping for Shoes

If you are serious about walking and intend to be building up your walking distance, it is worth giving some time and thought to buying the right shoe for you. One important factor in getting the right shoe can be finding the right sales person. It is a reality that many big box retailers and mall-based chains use young, low-paid and often inexperienced sales staff. Obviously there will be exceptions to this, but you are more likely to find a knowledgeable person in a specialist store. Usually these are stores that sell predominantly running and other sports shoes, but I've found that their staff will have often built up some expertise about walking shoes or will refer you to someone in the store who specializes in them. It's worth asking around by calling a local walking club or YM/YWCA about the

**10 More Walking Songs**

11. Why Walk When You Can Fly? (Mary Chapin Carpenter)
12. Walking the Dog (Rufus Thomas or Rolling Stones) (There was also a 60's hit called *Walking with my cat named Dog.*)
13. The Walk of Life (Dire Straits)
14. Walk Don't Run (Ventures)
15. Walking in a Winter Wonderland (Smith and Bernard)
16. Walking My Baby Back Home (Nat King Cole)
17. Walking to New Orleans (Fats Domino)
18. The Way I Walk (Jack Scott)
19. Walking (Willie Nelson, also Miles Davis)
20. You'll Never Walk Alone (Many versions including the Liverpool Soccer Fans)

best stores for your needs. A good salesperson, who knows their trade, will take into consideration most of the points that follow. Your own reading in this chapter will give you some of the questions to ask and a good salesperson will be able to provide informed answers.

If a salesperson tries to talk you into an uncomfortable shoe by saying something to the effect that it will feel better once it's *broken in* , say *thank you* and find another store.

### Buying a Walking Shoe: Things to Look For; Things to Avoid

1.  **Size wise.** The most common mistake people make when buying walking shoes (or any shoes) is that they don't allow enough room for the longest toes. (Note: This is usually the *big* toe but can also be its neighbor, the 4th toe, in what is called *Morten's foot*.) There should be a thumb-width, or about 1/2", between the end of your toe and the tip of your shoe. You should have room to wiggle your toes. If you ignore this rule you will regret it, because what can feel fine in the carpeted shoe store will soon be hurting and compressing your toes out on the street or the trails. Also, make sure that there is plenty of width and height for those precious toes. The overall length of the shoe is important, but there is another length to consider, namely the distance between the heel of the foot and the ball of the foot; what we refer to as the arch. It's important that your shoe fits your arch as well as your whole foot so that it bends and flexes in the same place your foot bends and flexes.
2.  The right time to shop for shoes is the end of the day. Feet swell during the day so that a shoe that might be 'just right' first thing in the morning is 'a bit tight' later in the day.
3.  Feet are rarely exactly the same, so make sure the shoe is right for your bigger foot. Also, don't assume you know what size to wear. Feet seem to spread as we age (mine have gone from a 9 1/2 to an 11). So never just buy by the numbers. To me this means that I would never get shoes by mail order.
4.  Your shoes should fit snugly around the heel to provide stability and not be a source of rubbing and irritation. Your heel should not slide around in the shoe.

*If high heels were so wonderful, men would be wearing them.*

Sue Grafton

*I still have my feet on the ground, I just wear better shoes.*

Oprah Winfrey

*My shoes are special shoes for discerning feet.*

Manolo Blahnik

5.  Before you buy the shoes make sure you take a walk in them on a hard surface. A carpeted floor can mask a number of deficiencies in a shoe.

6.  It's a good idea to stand on one foot, as that puts your full body weight on a single shoe. Check that there is no tightness or discomfort.

7.  If you wear orthotics or other customized inserts, make sure they are compatible with your new shoes before you purchase them. Also, take along your old walking shoes so your shoe salesperson can check for any unusual pattern of wear. Incidentally, a good shoe can sometimes be made even better by replacing the insole or sock-liner. It's surprising how many shoes costing over $100 have cheap, inadequate insoles. Talk to your qualified salesperson about the quality of the existing insole and whether it could be improved by purchasing an upgrade. A little more detail on orthotics is included later on in this chapter.

8.  Do your shoes rock? A well-designed walking shoe should have a slightly rounded or beveled heel. If you take a pencil and push down on the inside of the heel of the shoe, it should rock back, with the toe of the shoe coming off the ground.
    Likewise, if you push your finger on the toe of the shoe, the heel should lift off the ground. These design features enable you to have a smooth heel strike and a good spring from the toe.

9.  Not too much, not too little, but just right.
    The Goldilocks principle applies to flexibility in the shoe. The front part of the shoe should bend and flex easily, just as your foot does, but the center or arch support needs to be firm and stable. Likewise, there should be a certain amount of twist or lateral flexibility in your shoe. When walking, the foot rolls from the outside to the inside with each step and the cushioning and flexibility act like suspension in a car.

10. It can still look good. The better-looking the shoes, the more likely you are to wear them on a variety of occasions.

One question I'm asked from time to time is, *Can running shoes also be used as walking shoes?* The answer is *yes*. However, that doesn't mean that there is no difference between running shoes and walking shoes.

*After a day's walk everything has twice it's usual value.*

George Trevelyan

*Before supper, take a little walk.*
*After supper, do the same.*

Erasmus

(I)   Running shoes have more cushioning than walking shoes, because they have to absorb more than twice the force with each step.

For the next two segments I quote directly from Mark Fenton, editor at large for Walking Magazine and an expert in the biomechanics of walking. The quotes are from his excellent book, *A Complete Guide to Walking*.

(II)  *In the walking stride, your foot generally strikes the ground farther back on the heel, with the toes held higher up in the air, than in the running stride. The foot also rolls from heel to toe much more gradually in walking than in running. Thus a walking shoe should have a lower and more rounded or beveled heel than a running shoe. An extra-thick heel – needed to cushion high-impact running steps – acts only to lever the toes down quickly, which is bad for walking. In fact, a thick, squared-off running heel can even lead to shin discomfort for a brisk walker, because as the toes slap down, the foot pulls on the shin muscles. If your shins burn and you're walking briskly in running shoes, your first step should be to switch to walking shoes right away.*

(III) *A walker rolls farther off the toes at the end of each stride than a runner. So a walking shoe should be more flexible through the ball of the foot than a running shoe. Many running shoes trade flexibility for more padding (for shock absorption) in the front of the foot.*

I have provided you with a lot of details about feet and shoes, which to some readers might seem unnecessary. But remember, walking is a life giving, health enhancing activity, which provides pleasure and may well save you thousands of dollars in future medical bills. It's worth spending a bit of time and money to make sure you have the best shoes for the job.

This leads to one last question, *What are the best shoes?* There is an easy answer, but not a very helpful one. *The best shoe is the one that works for you.* Walking shoes seem a bit like computers, there's always a new, improved model coming out. Follow the directions and criteria in this chapter and you will be walking in a good pair of shoes. If you really like them, go back and buy another one or two pairs because, if you wait a few months and log over a million steps, the style that you liked so much may be discontinued.

*Between the saying and the doing, many a pair of shoes is worn out.*

Iris Murdoch

*We handicap horses by making them carry extra weight. We do the same thing to ourselves.*

Martin Collis

## Orthotics

Orthotics are inserts that are put in a shoe to supply some form of control, correction and support to the foot. They might have an arch support, designed to prevent something like overpronation. (Overpronation is when feet become unstable and roll inward and downward more than normal). Orthotics can help correct many problems associated with your feet. They are sometimes prescribed in response to chronic foot or leg pain, such as plantar fasciitis, shin splints, knee pain and other conditions. However, before you try to get a mechanical correction, consult a podiatrist, physiotherapist or sports medicine specialist to see if your problem can be cured by specific exercises and stretching, or maybe a change in walking technique.

Orthotics are a last resort. They should be custom made from a mold of your foot, so don't even think of buying cheap, ready-made ones off the shelf. They are expensive and have a mixed record of success. (I use them to help control a pronation problem and to protect a twice-broken arthritic big toe joint). If a problem persists and you've tried conservative methods of treatment, it might be time to see an expert and consider orthotics.

### Getting to Know Your Feet

There are one or two home tests where you can learn a little about you own feet, but these might be used more for personal interest than scientific accuracy.

Are your feet flexible, rigid or somewhere in between? Here's what you can do to help you answer this question and learn a bit more about your feet before you select a walking shoe.

Let's start with the flexibility test. You need a ruler and a chair. Sit in the chair and cross one leg over the opposite knee. Without pressing hard on the ruler measure the length of the elevated foot from heel to the tip of the longest toe. Record the measurement. Next, put the ruler on the floor and stand on it with the foot you've just measured. The weight of standing will produce some *spreading* of the foot. Record the same measurement from heel to toe.

- If the two measurements are about the same, your feet can be

### Healthier Than Thou

by Martin Collis

They're the fitness couple
For 2006
They think wellness too vital
To waste time having kicks.

He elliptically runs
She bikes and Bowflexes
She measures her strength
He checks his reflexes.

They're slim and attractive
Always on the run
And SPF careful
When out in the sun.

They drink Evian water
Their thirst to relieve
Although Evian backwards
Spells out naïve.

They text and they email
Their Internet friends
Cutting–edge zealots
Of technical trends.

And when at the age
Of one hundred and three
They move into
Cyberspace infinity.

There at the Pearly Gates
Saint Peter stands
She's a little surprised
They still use a man

He says, "Stop fitness family
You can't go through
Heaven's not structured
For people like you"

"But we've done it all right
We look almost new
We're healthy, AIDs free
And intelligent, too."

"Sorry" says Peter.
"You're not on the roll–call.
You've missed the big picture
By thinking too small.

Life's more than Pilates
And following trends
There's purpose, and meaning
And thoughts, which
transcend.

You're deficient in joy
And that's really tragic.
You can figure the tricks
But don't understand magic.

You're so self involved
And boring as well
I think you deserve
Some more years in Hell."

classed as *rigid*.

- If the measurements differ by about 0.32cm (1/8"), your feet can be classed as *neutral*.
- If the measurements differ by 0.64cm (1/4") or more, you can think of your feet as *flexible*.

The above produces a simple method of determining your foot type.

### Socks

The further you walk, the more socks can make a difference. On a short walk any regular sock will probably do the job, but if you start stepping out for longer walks socks, shoes and feet have got to get along together. Make sure your socks are the right size for your feet; avoid things like tube socks, especially ones made from cotton. The problem with cotton socks is that they tend to feel great when your feet are warm and dry, but as you sweat and the cotton absorbs moisture they can lose shape, wrinkle or bunch-up and can become an irritant rather than a smooth interface between shoe and foot. Virtually all socks sold in specialist stores for walkers and runners are made of modern synthetic fibers and have the ability to *wick* away moisture. Whether you like padded socks or thin socks is purely a matter of personal preference. My sock purchasing advice is similar to my advice about buying shoes. Find a good store, a salesperson whom you trust and get socks that feel good to you. If they continue to feel good when you're walking and after a few washings, pick up some extra pairs.

### Injuries

One of the reasons people like to walk, particularly older people, is that it is not an activity associated with injuries. Talk of injuries does tend to color writing about shoe selection and problems associated with cotton socks, but for the typical 10,000 stepper or the lunchtime walker injuries are almost a non-issue. For serious walkers that might walk a half or full marathon or take a hiking vacation, the main *injury* they're likely to encounter is a blister. Most of the time blisters can be avoided because the first symptom before a blister forms is a 'hot spot'. If you are able to cover the spot with a band-aid to stop the friction, or simply stop walking, a full blister can usually be avoided.

*The game was never worth a rap*
*For rational folks to play*
*In which no accident, no mishap,*
*Could ever find a way.*

Adam Gordon, 1936

*There is nothing like walking to get the feel of a*
*country. A landscape is like a piece of music, it*
*must be taken at the right tempo. Even a bicycle*
*can be too fast.*

Paul Scott Mowrer

If you are on a long walk there are a few ways to help blister-proof your feet.

(I)   Take along some extra socks so that you can change them when the ones you are wearing are wet and sweaty.
(II)  When you change your socks, dry your feet and allow them some time in the air.
(III) Powder your feet with cornstarch or a commercial foot powder, which will help absorb sweat and keep the friction down to a minimum.

Lastly, if you do develop a blister it should be carefully popped with a sterile needle and an antibiotic cream applied. If you need information about things such as corns, calluses, bunions, heel spurs, black toenails and other foot related problems I recommend an excellent book called *Walking Medicine* by Yanker and Burton.

*If you can't be a good example – then you'll just have to be a horrible warning.*

Unknown

*The quickest way to make yourself miserable is to stop keeping your agreements. Then you have to pretend you don't notice, or you have to tell lies or make excuses to cover yourself. Next thing you know you're in a ditch and you're not sure how you got there.*

Gail Padilla

# 11

# Stretch and Strength

The main theme of this book is walking, and how it relates to weight control and wellness. It's not primarily a book about flexibility and muscular performance. However, when I write about overall fitness I often frame it in terms of the "4 S's":

1) Stamina (Cardiovascular, pulmonary fitness)

2) Strength (Power, muscle tone and muscle endurance)

3) Suppleness (Flexibility)

4) Stability (Balance)

Walking is mostly associated with stamina and cardiovascular health, although the regular use of the feet, legs and postural muscles also contribute to stability. To develop all-round, functional fitness it's a good idea to pay some attention to strength and suppleness (the other 2 "S's") as a part of your overall wellness. In this chapter I will recommend a few simple stretches for the legs and some basic core muscle activation exercises, six strengthening activities and an introduction to using an

*Don't die with the music still in you.*

Emerson

*How you do anything is how you do everything.*

Anonymous

*Where your will is ready, your feet are light.*

George Herbert

exercise ball. At the end of the chapter you will find some references that can provide a lot more detail and variety about stretching, core work, exercise balls and strength training than this chapter allows.

**Note:** I sometimes add a 5^th S for *Shape*, which refers to body composition and contours.

### Stretching

### Why Stretch?

Regular stretching does more than help to maintain and improve suppleness. The benefits of stretching include:

(I)    Reduction of muscle tension, leading to feeling of relaxation.
(II)   Increased range of motion of joints.
(III)  Improved coordination as the body moves more fluidly.
(IV)   The development of body awareness.
(V)    Improved circulation.
(VI)   The body/mind works on a *use it or lose it* principle. Without regular stretching the body loses its ability to perform in various ways and might be vulnerable to injury if suddenly forced into challenging postures by accident or design.

Animals instinctively know that stretching is important and you don't have to be around a cat very long to see that stretching is a regular part of their built-in fitness routine. When you stretch in the right way it feels good, and goes on feeling good after you've finished. The key to success in stretching is the same as many other endeavors, do it correctly and do it often. Correctly means no forcing, bouncing, grimacing and trying to emulate performers in Cirque du Soleil. Correctly means relaxing into the stretch with the right technique and, in most cases, holding the position for up to 40 seconds. There's an old song titled, *You Can't Hurry Love* and the same applies to stretching; take your time, because *You Can't Hurry Stretching*. The suggested times for holding a stretch are approximations. In a well-executed stretch you will first isolate the muscle group until you feel some tension. Hold that position until the muscle *lets go* and relaxes. It can often take between 15 seconds and 25 seconds for this relaxation to occur. So use your own biofeedback rather than a stopwatch to define your time on each stretch.

*Hold fast to dreams*
*For if dreams die*
*Life is a broken-winged bird*
*That cannot fly.*

Langston Hughes

*You don't **grow** old.*
*You **get** old by not growing.*

E. Stanley Jones

There are many ways to appreciate the joy of flex, some seek it through yoga, others like to work with a fitness ball and other equipment, there's a lot of interesting stretching that can be done with a partner, but all you need for bread-and-butter daily stretching is a bit of space, a mat or other soft surface and a willingness to focus on the form and function of your own unique body.

### Walking and Stretching

It sounds like heresy, but you don't need to stretch before a walk in order to reduce the likelihood of injury. There are many studies that have looked at the correlation between pre-activity stretching and the incidence of injury and none have found significant correlations. It should be added, that the activity in these studies was a lot more challenging than walking and included marathon running and Australian military training. Many runners use walking itself to warm up their muscles and if you are going for a brisk walk you too can warm up by walking slowly at first. It is worth noting that muscles, ligaments and tendons are easier to stretch when they are warm and have good circulation, which means that if you are going to stretch, the logical time is after your walk, rather than before. Think of muscles being like chewing gum, which you can't really stretch easily until it has been chewed on and *warmed up*.

### Stretching Guidelines

As noted above, warm up before you stretch. My students used to be surprised when I'd give them a sit and reach test before and after a run. They'd always be able to reach an extra 2 or 3 inches (5 – 7.5cm) after their run.

Breathe out when going into a stretch and breathe in when coming out of a stretch. Remember OUT going in and IN coming out.

NEVER stretch to a point of feeling pain!! A little discomfort, *yes*, but pain, *no*.

Unlike strength training, you can stretch the same muscles every day.

*I run on the road, long before I dance under the lights.*

Muhammad Ali

*Energy is not lost by exertion, but maintained by it.*

Germaine Greer

Note: I think Germaine was only partly correct. In most cases energy is not just *maintained* by exercise and exertion, it is *increased*.

### Exercise Illustrations

To get perfect form in every picture it would have been easy for us to import yoga practitioners, fitness leaders or young exercise models. However, one rule in writing this book was that we would not include activities that we don't practice ourselves. (Whether we practice what we preach, or preach what we practice is debatable). To this end I chose to have my wife Nancy and executive assistant Bev act as models for the various stretch and strength activities featured in the book. We expect you, the reader, to be involved and, as Albert Schweitzer said, *Example isn't the best teacher, it's the only teacher.*

### Acknowledgement

In selecting and describing many of the following exercises I worked with medical exercise specialist, Rich Gafter-Ricks. Rich runs a company called Exercise Partners and specializes in working in conjunction with his client's physicians, surgeons, therapists or other health professionals to maximize the benefits of their rehabilitation or other designated programs. I see Rich as an interface between the instructions of the medical professionals and the real world. Rich is a Certified Medical Exercise Program Director among his many qualifications, but his real strength lies in creating challenging programs that keep his clients on track or on task. I feel that many rehab and prevention programs fail because people don't have access to someone with Rich's focus and qualifications

### Six of the Best

### Leg Stretches

I.  **Calf Stretch** Lean forward from the hips and brace your hands against a wall. Take a half step forward with the left foot so that the left heel is under the hip. Slide the right foot back, but keep the heel on the ground. [fig.1] Lean forward, bending the elbows and making sure that the right heel stays on the ground. You will feel in increased tension and stretch in the calf muscle (the gastrocnemius). [fig.2]

fig.1

*It was the best of times*
*And the worst of times,*
*It was the age of wisdom*
*And the age of foolishness.*

Charles Dickens

Dickens' words still ring true today.

It's the age of the jogger and the age of the couch potato.
We spend billions on diets and have never been fatter.
There are record sales of anti-depressants and record levels of long-term disability for depression.
Most women's magazines feature models wearing size 2 or 4 outfits, the most common dress size is 14.
Labor saving devices abound, we've never been busier.
There are now three fat people for every two starving people, which sounds like the worst of times and the worst of times.

fig.2                         fig.3

Variation: (Soleus stretch)
Still using the same stance against the wall but bending the right knee (rear leg) about 20° will enable you to stretch the soleus muscle, which lies under the gastrocnemius. [fig3] Both stretches also stretch the Achilles tendon. Hold each stretch for 40 seconds or until you feel the muscle release. Repeat with the leg positions reversed.

**2.  Hamstring Stretch**
The typical North American has a real imbalance in their thigh muscles, with the quads (large muscles in the front of the thigh) being disproportionately stronger than the hamstrings. Strengthening and stretching the hamstrings have a number of benefits. Stretching the hamstrings often relieves low back discomfort and protects you from lower back problems. It also stretches the soft tissue around your sciatic nerve and gives you greater range of body motion.

Lie on your back with knees bent, feet flat on the mat and arms by your sides with the hands palms down. Tighten your abdominals, stretch out the back of your neck and press your lower back into the mat. Try to maintain this throughout the stretch. [fig.4]

*We are what we repeatedly do.*

Aristotle

*Blessed are the flexible for they*
*shall not be bent out of shape.*

Sue Petrie Marsh

fig.4

Keep the left foot on the mat with the knee bent and raise the right leg up until the thigh is at about a 90° angle to your body. Keep the right knee bent. Wrap a belt under the arch of the right foot, holding either end of the belt with each hand. [fig.5]

fig.5

Pull on the belt to help straighten your right leg towards the sky or ceiling. Feel the stretch behind your right thigh and knee. Using a belt or towel helps keep the calf muscles relaxed. Hold the stretch until you feel the loss of tension in the muscle as it releases. [fig.6]

fig.6

Repeat with the leg positions reversed.

## Words Of Wisdom

by Donald Ardell, Ph.D.

From the Electronic Ardell Wellness Report
Issue #43 — September 22, 2000

### TEN TIPS FOR WELLNESS

1  YOU'RE IN CHARGE! Advice can come from many sources but ultimately it is your choices that most affect the quality of your health and life.

2  SEEK A WAY TO GET PAID TO DO WHAT YOU ENJOY. It is very difficult to be well if you can't express your talents and passions at work, in some manner.

3  CHANGE IS THE NORM-DEAL WITH IT. Coming to terms with the fact that change is inevitable and happening at a faster pace than ever before will help you deal more effectively with the fact that nothing stays the same.

4  DOCTORS AND DRUGS ARE OVERRATED. Your lifestyle choices, including your attitudes/beliefs/emotional responses and actions, have more impact on your health than doctors, medications, the economy, your income level, your age, your employer or your luck.

5  FUN IS SERIOUS. Wellness is too important to be pursued grimly. Whatever your choices, make sure you're having fun.

6  MODERN MEDICINE IS GOOD BUT. Modern medicine's a wonderful thing BUT there are two problems: people expect too much of it and too little of themselves.

7  EXCELLENCE TRUMPS BALANCE. Balance is good but there are times when you have to put it aside to pursue a passion or heroic quest.

8  DON'T GIVE UP ANYTHING! At least not initially, as it is better to take up healthy practices than to give up unhealthy habits, at least initially when trying to enhance the quality of your lifestyle. **For example, you are better advised to take up a satisfying activity like vigorous walking before you attempt to quit smoking.**

9  EXCELLENCE IS NO ACCIDENT. Lifestyle quality or an advanced state of well being is seldom achieved by accident—you have to make a choice to live and work this way.

10  THERE IS STILL TIME. It's never too late to start a wellness lifestyle—while alive. Or, stated another way, "Exercise vigorously every day until you die when, for the first time in your life, it won't matter anymore.

Good luck. Enjoy and be as well as possible.

Visit Don Ardell's website at **http://www.seekwellness.com/wellness/**

3.    **IT Stretch** Stretch for the gluteus maximus, IT band (Iliotibial band) and the smaller muscles of the external hip rotators.

The IT band, which runs along the outer part of your thigh and connects to the gluteus maximus, is a difficult tendonous structure to stretch. It is important to maintain its range however, because IT band syndrome is difficult to treat and can cause a lot of discomfort.

Start by lying on your back on the mat in a similar starting position to Stretch 2 (Hamstring Stretch). [fig.4]

Keeping the right leg in the bent leg starting position, bring the left knee up towards your chest and hook the left foot behind the right knee. [fig.7]

fig.7

Now draw your right foot towards your butt, feeling the stretch in the left side of your butt and down the outside of your left thigh.

Finally, clasp both hands behind the right thigh and pull it in towards your chest, lifting the right foot off the floor. This will increase the intensity of the stretch, but remember, stretch through discomfort but not pain. [figs8 and 9]

figs.8 and 9

*The doctor of the future will give no medicine, but instead will interest his patients in the care of the human frame, in diet, and in the cause and prevention of disease.*

Thomas Edison

Note: Good idea Thomas but it hasn't happened yet.

*We sit at breakfast, we sit in the car, we sit at work, we sit at lunch, we sit all afternoon then drive home and sit in front of a screen, a hodgepodge of sagging livers, sinking gall bladders, dropping stomachs, compressed intestines and squashed pelvic organs.*

John Button Jr.

## 4. Quad Stretch
### Lying Quad Stretch

Lie on your stomach with your head resting on your left forearm. [fig.10]

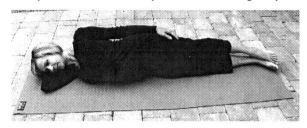

fig.10

Keeping your knees together, gently pull your right heel towards your butt until you feel the stretch in your quads (front thigh or quadriceps muscle). It's best to grasp your leg on, or just above, your ankle. Hold the stretch until the muscle 'lets go' and the feeling of tension is gone. [figs.11 and 12]

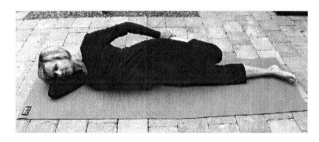

figs.11 and 12

### Standing Quad Stretch

You often see runners and soccer players doing a few standing quad stretches before entering the fray of competition. They usually don't hold the stretch long enough to accomplish anything.

Stand erect and raise the right heel towards the right buttock, keeping your knees together. Grasp the leg in the same way as in the lying stretch. You can use the left hand to steady yourself against a wall if necessary. Again, hold the stretch long enough until the muscle 'lets go'. If you can do this without support it is a good balance exercise. [fig.13]

fig.13

*The human body is made up of some four hundred muscles; evolved through centuries of physical activity. Unless these are used, they will deteriorate.*

Eugene Lyman Fisk

*The human body is a machine, which winds its own springs.*

J.O. de la Mettrie

### 5. Groin Stretch

This actively stretches the adductor muscles that draw your legs together. Sit comfortably erect either in an open area or with your back against a wall and your knees bent. [fig.14]

fig.14                                    fig.15

Allow the knees to fall apart and place the soles of your feet together. Place your hands on the inside of your knees and gently press down. [fig.15 ] Make sure you maintain pressure evenly on each side. After you feel the initial tension hold the stretch until the muscle relaxes.

### 6. Hip Flexors

Technically, what is often called the *runners' stretch* is not a stretch, but a very good mobilization of the hips. Take a step forward with your left leg so that the knee is about 90°. Lower the right knee towards the ground, keeping the upper body still as you push your hips forward. You should feel the tension in the front of the right hip. [fig.16]

fig.16

As for exercise of the body which is the subject of the ensuing discourse, if people would not think so superficially of it, if they would but abstract the benefit got by it from the means by which it is got, they would set a great value on it. If some of the advantages accruing from exercise were to be procured by any one medicine, nothing in the world would be in more esteem than that medicine would be. There is this difference between the most complete productions of human artifice and that fine piece of mechanism – the human body; that the former are always the worst for wearing and decay by use in motion, the latter, notwithstanding the tenderness of its contexture, improves by exercise and acquires by frequent motion an ability to last the longest.

Francis Fuller, MD (1705)

## Basic Core Muscle Activation Exercises

The author of this series of exercises is Dr. Rob Hasegawa, who is a meticulous, conservative chiropractor and, incidentally, is a national champion triathlete for his age group. One of the reasons for Rob's professional and athletic success is his complete understanding of the human body, which gives him an ability to diagnose and treat injuries and imbalances in his patients and to use his limited training time to maximum advantage. The body's 'core' includes the trunk, pelvis, hips, abdominal muscles and the small muscles along the spinal column. Dr. Hasegawa developed a series of 5 simple exercises, which he likes many of his patients to do to reinforce his treatments. However, everyone can benefit from these simple activities, particularly people that might be dealing with some form of lower back pain or weakness.

These exercises should be done lying on the floor on a thin carpet. They are to be done slowly and with good control. Breathe slowly and deeply, inhaling when muscles are relaxing and exhaling when muscles are contracting. Closing your eyes and visualizing the movements and muscles involved will enhance the effectiveness of these exercises.

Do each exercise 12 times.

Aim to do these core activation exercises at least 3 times a week. It will take about 5 minutes a session. If you can do them every day it's even better.

**1.  Pelvic Tilt**
Lie on your back with your knees bent up and heels near your buttocks, arms at your sides, palms down. [fig.1] Contract your lower abdominal muscles while you exhale, and push your spine towards the ground, flattening it out. Hold, then release the contraction as you inhale. [fig.2]

fig.1

fig.2

### The 8 Rules For Being Human

1. You will receive a body. You may like it, you may hate it, but it will be yours for the entire period this time around. You can keep it well fed and exercised, or abuse it. The choice is yours.

2. You will learn lessons. You are enrolled in a full-time informational school called life. Each day in this school you will learn lessons. You may like the lessons or think them irrelevant and hence choose to ignore them, no matter, keep reading.

3. A lesson is repeated until learned. It will be presented to you in various forms until you have learned it. Once learned, you will then go on to the next lesson.

4. There are no mistakes, only lessons. Growth is a process of trial and error; experimentation. The *failed* experiments are as much a part of the process as the experiment that ultimately *works*.

5. Learning lessons does not end. There is no part of life that dos not contain its lesson. If you are alive, there are lessons to be learned.

6. *There* is no better than *here*. When your *there* has become a *here* you will simply obtain another *there* that will again look better than *here*.

7. Your answers lie only inside you. The answers to life's questions lie only inside you. All you need to do is look, listen, and trust.

8. You will forget all this.

## 2. Hip Shrug

Lie on your back, legs straight and arms at your side. [fig.3]

fig.3                    fig.4                    fig.5

Exhale and slowly pull one hip up towards the armpit on the same side by contracting the muscle deep in your back just above your belt line. [fig.4] Hold and then release the contraction, inhale, and repeat with the other hip. [fig.5]

## 3. Toe Out Leg Raise

Lie on your back, legs straight, and arms at your sides. [fig.6]

fig.6

Roll one leg outward, exhale, and slowly lift it up towards the ceiling. Pause and hold it for a moment before lowering it slowly to the ground. Repeat with the other leg. [fig.7]

fig.7

*When health is absent*
*Wisdom cannot reveal itself*
*Art cannot become manifest*
*Strength cannot be exerted*
*Wealth is useless and*
*Reason powerless.*

Herophilies, 300bc

*No great thing is created suddenly.*

Epictetus

### 4. Side Leg Raise

Lie on your side with your legs straight and on top of each other. Keep your hips stacked on top of each other by rolling slightly forward. Do not roll backwards. [fig.8]

fig.8

Slowly raise the upward leg to 45 degrees as you exhale [fig.9], pause, and then lower it slowly back down. Do 12, then roll over and do the other leg.

fig.9

### 5. Mule Kick

Start on your hands and knees with a flat, stable back. [fig.10]

fig.10                              fig.11

Slowly raise one heel and push it back as you straighten your leg. Pause, then bring it back down and lift and straighten the other leg. [fig.11]

233

*We are under-exercised as a nation.*
*We look instead of play.*
*We ride instead of walk.*
*Our existence deprives us*
*of the minimum of physical activity*
*essential for healthy living.*

John F. Kennedy

*He/she not busy being born,*
*is busy dying.*

Bob Dylan

## Strength

If you don't use muscles you lose them and some specific strengthening work makes sense if you wish to maintain and increase the strength and endurance potential of your muscles. Muscles burn calories, so an additional benefit to doing some strength training is that your body burns more calories. As important as anything is that being strong is a good feeling that invariably adds to your sense of well-being. I used to teach a required fitness and conditioning class to university students. What amazed them was not how hard it was, but how quickly they could build strength and endurance. Many students started the class unable to do a push-up; chin-up or bar dip and 12 weeks later could do multiple repetitions of all of them. I absolutely guarantee that if you regularly challenge your muscles with strengthening exercises **you will get stronger.** This guarantee applies to any age group. Westcott et al. administered a strength-training program to elderly nursing home patients and after a 14-week program reported strength gains of over 80%. In a one year, twice weekly program for post-menopausal women studied at Tufts University strength increased 75%, dynamic balance improved 13% and bone density, instead of declining, actually increased 1%. It's never too late to get strong.

### Six of the Best

With no machines, weights or special equipment.

### 1. Push Ups

Push-ups have a bad reputation. Misguided physical education teachers and coaches often used them as punishment. Some of you might have experienced the feeling of humiliation when you weren't able to execute even one push-up in a group situation. Many people have left school or the military with the thought, *I'll never have to do another push-up in my life*. You don't *have* to, but now you're wiser, you might *want* to.
The good old push-up develops muscles in the chest, shoulders, arms (triceps) and even the back.

**Modified Push-Up**
If you are unable to do a classic, full-body push-up, start with the modified version. Kneel on the mat and place your hands on the mat, shoulder width apart. [fig.1]

fig.1

235

*A person who fears suffering – is already suffering from what they fear.*

Montaigne

*Certainties are arrived at only on foot.*

Antonio Porchia

Keeping your upper body and neck straight, lower yourself to within an inch or two of the mat and then straighten the arms to raise your upper body and trunk, using your knees as a fulcrum. [fig.2]

fig.2

When you can do 15 controlled, modified push-ups you're ready for the classic push-up.

### Classic Push-Up

Hands on the mat, shoulder width apart. Extend your legs until your body is straight, with the toes curled under. [fig.3]

fig.3

Tighten your tummy muscles so you avoid sagging or arching your back. Then, keeping your body straight, bend at the elbows and lower the body towards the mat. Don't collapse on the mat, but stop short and extend the arms until you are back to the starting position and ready for the next complete classic push-up. Work up to 15 repetitions.

One of the important things that many North Americans have lost is the ability to control their own body weight. Unless you strengthen your arms and shoulders they will become like the wings of penguins, not very useful.

### 2. The Karate Squat

The squat develops the muscle groups which are so important in the activities of daily living. Actions such as sitting down, standing up, lifting and pulling are all facilitated by leg strength and a stable core. Likewise, climbing and descending stairs and steep hills comes more easily when your legs are strong.

Rather than have the arms do nothing in this exercise, we added a series of karate like punches to activate the muscles of the shoulders and upper arms.

*There's no one to beat you, no one to defeat you,*
*Except the thoughts of yourself feeling bad.*

Bob Dylan

*How old would you be if you didn't know how old*
*you were?*

Satchel Paige

fig.4

Stand with your feet hip width apart. Tuck both elbows next to your ribs. Make two fists. [fig.4] As you squat down, punch out with your right arm, and as you stand up, bring your right elbow back to the side of your ribs. [fig.5] Repeat the same pattern on the next squat, punching with your left arm instead of your right. Repeat the alternating squat punches 15 times per side.

fig.5

3. **The Dead Bug** (right to the core)

This is a famous core activity with an inappropriate name. It more closely resembles a very live bug, such as a beetle, stuck on its back with its legs waving in the air. This is a great exercise for strengthening the pelvic floor. It strengthens the muscles, which support the bladder and rectum, and improves the function of those organs. Over time, this activity will do more for your abdominals than sit-ups or crunches.

Lie on your back with your knees bent at 90 degrees. [fig.6]

fig.6

Raise your arms directly overhead and reach for the ceiling. Keep your lower back pressed into the floor at all times.

239

*I re-entered my life, through re-entering my body.*

George Sheehan

*I know that Robert Frost was right. I have
promises to keep and miles to go before I sleep.*

George Sheehan

Now bring your knees up and your feet off the floor until your thighs are vertical, with knees bent at about 90 degrees. Extend the right leg forward followed by a straight right arm almost as though it is attached by a string to the right knee. The legs now begin a gentle 'cycling' motion and, as the right knee

fig.7

comes back, the left leg begins to extend, 'pulling' the left arm with it [fig.7] Keep the back pressed to the mat. Continue alternately extending and 'cycling' the legs with straight arms following each leg as it extends. You will feel the exercise very deep into your abdominals. Perform 15 per side. The lower you move your leg, the more advanced the exercise. You decide how low to the ground your leg can be, as long as your lower back stays on the floor.

## 4. **Heel Raises**
This simple exercise strengthens the calf muscles; the gastrocnemius and the soleus. It can be done flat on the floor or on a small raised block or step to get a greater range of movement in the ankle.

Stand with your feet slightly apart, toes pointing forward. [fig8] Push the toes down so that the heel rises up and the calf muscles contract. [fig.9] This might seem easy at first, but as you add repetitions you'll quickly experience that your calf muscles are working hard.

fig.8          fig.9

*The hardest years in life are those
between ten and seventy.*

Helen Hayes (at 73)

*Last week I saw a woman who hasn't
made a mistake in 3000 years. She was a
mummy in the Metropolitan Museum.*

Christine Menzel

The heel raise can be made more challenging by lifting one foot off the ground and hooking it behind the ankle of the other leg. [figs.10 and 11] Then proceed to do some single leg, heel raises. [fig.12]

| fig.10 | fig.11 | fig.12 |

This activity not only strengthens your calf muscles, but also stretches them along with your Achilles tendon. Strength in this area will help improve walking mechanics with a better heel strike and toe off.

5. **Thigh Tighteners** (Glutes, quads and hamstrings)
Lie on your back, using a small neck support if necessary for comfort. Place about a 6-inch (15cm) roll under your knees, such as a towel or mat. [fig.13] Tighten the right hamstrings and quads followed by the right buttock to press the back of the right knee down onto the supporting roll. [fig.14] Hold the contraction for 10 seconds and then relax and switch to the other leg. Build up to 15 repetitions.

fig.13

fig.14

*90% of life is showing up.*

Woody Allen

*It's not that I'm afraid to die; I just don't want to be there when it happens.*

Woody Allen

This exercise is almost an isometric contraction with little actual movement of the thigh. By strengthening the muscles of your thighs you get functional benefits in performing the activities of daily living; you get tighter, more shapely thighs and, very importantly, you build up the muscle around your knees to help protect your knee joint.

**Part 2 The Thigh Squeeze**
Lie on your back, knees bent and feet flat on the floor. Place a rolled mat, towel or ball between your knees. [fig.15] Squeeze your knees together so that the muscles on the inside of your thighs, the adductors, are fired and strengthened. [fig.16] Hold for a count of 6, and build up to 15 repetitions.

fig.15                              fig.16

Regulars at the gym often refer to the adductors as the 'sex muscles'. In reality, a well-trained, strong body heightens the sexual experiences for both partners.

## 6. Chair Dips
This is a challenging exercise, which develops the muscles of the upper body, shoulders and upper arms. (Pectorals, 'lats', deltoids and triceps). The only piece of equipment you need is a chair.

Sit on the chair, placing your hands on the front of the chair seat either side of your legs. Then, holding the hands in position, move your butt forward off the chair with legs stretched out in front of you in an L-sit position. [fig.17]

fig.17

*First say to yourself, what would you be; and then do what you have to do.*

Epictetus

*Don't count the days, make the days count.*

Muhammad Ali

Now, lower the butt towards the floor allowing the elbows to bend, controlling the dip with you upper body and arms. [fig.18] Push back and repeat. Avoid bouncing and jerky movements.

This is a challenging movement and some people find it easier to use two chairs and do the dip in between them. The dip is another of those important exercises that

fig.18

informs you how well you can control your own body weight with your arms. If you can't do one dip use a friend to help you by taking some of your weight while the arms build up strength. Work up to a goal of 15 dips.

### Afterword

I have provided a few simple strengthening exercises, but have only scratched the surface of the strength-training world. Gymnasia and fitness studios are full of barbells, dumbbells, pulleys and machines, which you may or may not feel comfortable using. There is a big pay-off in looks, performance, bone strength and confidence in strengthening the musculature of your body. A significant part of the success of the Curves organization is that they have created an environment where women feel comfortable doing regular strength training as part of a brisk half hour workout.

Remember, muscles not used, or muscles underused get weak and non-functional. Think what happens to the muscles of a leg that has been in a cast for only a few weeks. The muscles almost disappear and have to be rehabilitated by strength training. There is a huge pay-off to simple strength training, which makes a great addition to your 10,000 steps.

### The Exercise Ball

In recent years, the exercise ball (also known as the Swiss ball, physioball, fitness ball and stability ball) has gone mainstream. It's hard to find a gym, fitness studio, rehab facility or training center that doesn't feature exercise balls. The ball had its roots in therapy and rehabilitation, but various practitioners quickly discovered that the exercise ball was

*If you had to identify, in one word, the reason why the human race has not achieved, and never will achieve its full potential, that word would be 'meetings'.*

Dave Barry

*No matter what happens, someone will find a way to take it too seriously.*

Dave Barry

wonderful for core strengthening, flexibility, balance and injury prevention. The ball has many advantages, which include:

1. It is inexpensive.
2. It requires virtually no maintenance.
3. It can be used individually at home or in a group setting.
4. It can be adapted for use by all ages and fitness levels from seniors to national caliber athletes.
5. It can be used in place of a chair at work, providing ongoing stimulation for the balancing and postural muscles.

I use an exercise ball, but don't consider myself an expert, so I sought out the expertise of three young men who live in my hometown of Victoria and who have written the definitive book on the use of the exercise ball titled *Ball Bearings: The Complete Illustrated Guide of Ball Exercises*™ (www.ballbearings.org). Jeff Compton is a Certified Strength and Conditioning Specialist, Stefan Scott has worked in the training and rehabilitation of athletes and coordinates the Human Anatomy labs at the University of Victoria and Matthew Tyler is a physiotherapist working primarily with sports and orthopedic injuries. *Ball Bearings*™ is clearly written, easy to use and fun to read because of the insights and sense of humor of the authors. So let's play ball.

### What to look for when buying a ball

Look for a ball that is 'burst resistant'. This does *not* mean the ball is puncture proof but *does* mean that if there is a puncture that the air will leak out slowly, as opposed to whooshing out and dumping you on the floor. Look for a ball that will support at least 500lbs (225kg).

Balls typically come in three diameters, 55cm (21in), 65cm (25in) and 75cm (29in). The best guide in choosing the ball for you is comfort, so do a little checking before you buy. You should be in a position with your knees and hips bent at approximately 90°. Minor comfort adjustments can be made by inflating or deflating the ball slightly until you have that Goldilocks *just right* position.

*The generic drug is exercise, you must find your own particular brand.*

George Sheehan

*Sweat cleanses from the inside, it comes from places a shower will never reach.*

George Sheehan

## Safety

Some ball exercises can be challenging to the back and neck. If you have an injury or weakness in your spine, consult with a medical professional before doing ball work. With careful progressions and professional guidance the exercise ball ultimately becomes an ideal medium for strengthening the core of the body and the function of the muscles in your back and neck. Common sense and care are always an important part of any conditioning program.

### Six of the best on the ball

**Note**: In describing the following six exercises I will sometimes refer to your TVA. This is an abbreviation for Transversus Abdominis, which is one of the major spinal stabilizers, which play a key role in core stability. To contract your TVA, hollow your lower abdomen, *especially the sides*, using only 20% to 30% of your maximum contraction. This is not as easy as it might sound. To help you visualize what to do, or contract, try one of the points below.

- Try to pull the corners of your pelvis (the hard, boney points) towards each other.
- Imagine pulling the sides of your waist away from your belt.

It takes a lot of practice to gain complete control of your core stabilizers.

The *neutral position* referred to in some of the following exercises is simply sitting upright on the ball, with your feet flat on the floor, slightly wider than shoulder width apart and hands resting on your thighs. Sit with your shoulders down and back, chest out (naturally, not like a caricature) and keep the head up with ears over your shoulders.

Engage your TVA and low back muscles and allow your spine to keep its natural alignment; breathe normally.

Neutral position

*Life is the great experiment. Each of us is
an experiment of one – observer and subject –
making choices, living with them,
recording the effects.*

George Sheehan

*Nothing is good or bad, but thinking makes it so.*

William Shakespeare

## 1. One Legged Statue

The benefits of this exercise come from the torso and hips maintaining a neutral spine while simultaneously improving balance, muscle coordination and core stability. Like many ball activities a variety of muscle groups are involved including postural muscles, lower trunk, hips, pelvis, quads and shoulders.

Begin with a neutral spine posture. Hold your arms out to the side, parallel to the ground, for balance. [fig.1] Focus on stabilizing your core by contracting your core stabilizing muscles. Be careful not to lean back. Using a slow and controlled movement, raise one leg straight out in front of you and hold for 5 seconds. [fig.2]

fig.1

Alternate legs. Begin with 5 repetitions of each leg for 5 seconds and gradually work up to holding for 10 seconds.

fig.2

## 2. Walk Out

The Walk Out actually takes you into the starting position for many ball exercises. It targets the low back, Transversus Abdominis (TVA), buttocks, hips and quads.

Start in the neutral spine seated position. [fig.3] Slowly walk your feet forward while leaning back into the ball. Place your hands on the ball for added stability. [fig.4] Continue forward until your head and neck rest on the ball.

fig.3

*Don't take anyone else's definition of success as your own.*

Jacqueline Brisken

*A committee is a cul-de-sac down which good ideas are lured and then quietly strangled.*

Sir Barnett Cocks

fig.5

fig.4

Keep your hips up, don't sag, remember your neutral spine. In the 'Finish' position, engage your TVA but keep your abs relaxed. [fig.5]

To return to a seated position, contract your abs, bring your chin to your chest and walk your feet back towards the ball.
Initially try to hold the Finish position for 15 seconds.

### 3. Pelvic Shimmy

The Pelvic Shimmy will help improve the dynamic control and range of motion of your lower trunk and hips. It targets the muscles of the lower trunk including, the obliques, low back and buttocks.

Start in the neutral sitting posture. [fig.6] Shimmy your hips from side to side. [figs.7 and 8]

fig.6

fig.7

fig.8

*Nothing in the world can take the place of persistence. Talent will not; nothing is more common than unsuccessful men with talent. Genius will not; unrewarded genius is almost a proverb. Education will not; the world is full of educated derelicts. Persistence and determination alone are omnipotent. The slogan 'press on' has solved and always will solve the problems of the human race.*

Calvin Coolidge

*Happiness comes with effort; it is not a vicarious experience. We find, or come upon happiness through activity.*

George Sheehan

Next, tilt your pelvis backwards and forwards, going from a pelvic tilt plus position forward with the buttocks rolling under the spine. [figs.9 and 10] Your butt will move forwards and backwards on top of the ball. Keep your upper body (chest, shoulders and head) as still as possible while the hips are active.

Start with 30 seconds of the pelvic shimmy and work up to 90 seconds.

figs.9 and 10

## 4. **The Bridge**

This improves core strength and stability and targets the hamstrings, buttocks, low back, upper back and shoulders.

Lie on your back, arms spread wide, hands palms up and place your heels on the ball. [fig.11] Engage your TVA and slowly raise your hips upward until your body is straight. [fig.12] To help maintain balance, use your hands and arms, which adds a challenge to your upper back and shoulders.

fig.11                    fig.12

*Minds, like bodies, will often fall into
a pimpled, ill-conditioned state from
mere excess of comfort.*

Charles Dickens

*It is remarkable how one's wits are
sharpened by physical exercise.*

Pliny the Younger

As you get tired, your hips will tend to sag; try to prevent this! However, be careful to avoid arching your hips too far towards the ceiling: so do not push up beyond your neutral spine position.

The progression is to use your hands less and less by moving them closer to your body. Ultimately you might be able to keep them off the floor by crossing them on your chest.
Start by trying 5 repetitions of 10 seconds each and work up to 10 reps.

### 5. Ball Squeeze

This exercise strengthens your inner thighs. Start in a neutral seated posture with your legs straddling the ball, arms held out horizontal for balance. [fig.13]

fig.13

Keeping your toes in contact with the ground, squeeze the ball with your inner thighs and knees. As you do this your body will rise. Hold the squeeze for about 5 seconds and relax. [fig.14]

While you perform this exercise try to maintain your neutral posture. Start with 6 repetitions of 5 seconds each and work up to 12 reps.

fig.14

### 6. Ball Crunches

The ball crunch will help increase abdominal strength and flexibility. In addition to the abs, the neck is also part of this exercise.

Use the 'walk out' (#2 ball exercise) to get in to the start position. Cross your hands on your chest and push your tongue against the roof of your mouth to activate your deep neck muscles. [fig.15]

With a slow and controlled pace, use your abdominal muscles to curl

*Life is either a daring adventure or nothing.*

Helen Keller

your upper body as if you are trying to make your chest and belly button meet, rising up until your shoulder blades come off the ball. [fig.16] Pause for a second, then slowly return to the Start position and repeat.

fig.15                                                            fig.16

Do not bounce on the ball or use the ball to 'rebound' yourself back up. You must keep your low back in contact with the ball at all times. The ball should not move during this exercise. Progress by rolling yourself further back over the ball to start.

Try six repetitions and work up until you can do 30.

### Resources

Books that will help you get the most out of your workouts for stretching, strength work and core conditioning.

---

**Ball Bearings: The Complete Illustrated Guide of Ball Exercises™**
by J. Compton, S. Scott and M. Tyler

Anyone who owns or uses a fitness ball should have this book. We sell hundreds of *Ball Bearings*™ at Speakwell and have had nothing but positive feedback. It contains over 100 exercises to maximize strength and stability and shows that you can get a complete body workout with the exercise ball as your only piece of equipment. This book is used by experts and beginners and it would be hard to improve on its presentation and content. With its large format and graphics the Ball Bearings activities are even easier to follow than those shown above.

---

*Cripple him, and you have a Sir Walter Scott. Lock him in a prison cell, and you have a John Bunyan. Bury him in the snows of Valley Forge, and you have a George Washington. Raise him in abject poverty, and you have an Abraham Lincoln. Strike him down with infantile paralysis, and he becomes Franklin Roosevelt. Burn him so severely that the doctors say he'll never walk again, and you have a Glenn Cunningham – who set the world's one mile record in 1934. Deafen him, and you have a Ludwig van Beethoven. Have him or her born black in a society filled with racial discrimination, and you have a Booker T. Washington, a Marian Anderson, a George Washington Carver. Call him a slow learner, "retarded," and write him off as uneducable, and you have an Albert Einstein. As one man summed it up: Life is about 20% in what happens to us and 80% in the way we respond to the events.*

Ted Engstrom

**The Core Program** by Peggy Brill

Medical exercise specialist, Rich Gafter-Ricks, feels that 'The Core Program' is *the* core program. This book is designed for women, but having worked through many of the activities on a daily basis, I can assure you that it has plenty of challenge and applicability for men. Descriptions, illustrations and progressions are all first class. There is a useful section on weight training at the end of the book.

**Stretching** by Bob and Jean Anderson

This book was self-published some 25 years ago and since then has sold millions of copies. It has now been revised and updated with new drawings and 11 new everyday routines (eg airplane stretches, computer and desk stretches, stretches for kids). The book is very comprehensive and easy to use.

**The Stark Reality of Stretching** by Steven Stark

A remarkably good book, which presents the theory and practice of stretching with crystal clear understanding. Dr. Stark shows why some favorite stretches are inappropriate and, in some cases, damaging. I've learned a lot from this book, which is now in its 4th edition.

**Strength Training for Beginners** by S. Dinan and J. Bassey

The target audience for this book is women aged 35 and up with little experience of strength training.

**Strength Training Past 50** by W. Westcott and T. Baechle

Westcott and Baechle are world renowned experts in this area and have put together the definitive book on strength training for seniors.

**The Little Strength Training Book** by Erika Dillman

The author presents a practical book, which includes good background information on the theory and safety of strength training. The strength training programs are easy to follow and well presented.

*All beginnings are hard.*

Spanish proverb

*There is no finish line.*

Nike advertisement

*You already have everything you
need to be a long-distance athlete.
It's mind-set, not miles, that separate
those who do from those who dream.*

John Bingham

# 12

# Beyond 10,000

### Walking a Marathon

The first time I saw the Honolulu Marathon I was struck by the huge number of participants wearing purple t-shirts. On closer inspection, the shirts were inscribed "Leukemia and Lymphoma Society's Team-In-Training". The Honolulu Marathon begins at 5am and the elite runners are pouring across the finish line between 7 and 8am. The purple t-shirts start to show up at the finish line from about 11am onward and continue to walk to the finish throughout the rest of the day, some in good shape and others clearly the worse for wear.

All those purple shirts are the result of a brilliant fundraising scheme run by The Leukemia and Lymphoma Society. They select various walker-friendly marathons and will train you and pay your airfare and hotel for the event. You are expected to cover these costs and more by getting people to sponsor you. In this way, thousands of people have learned that they can walk the 26-plus miles (42k) of a marathon and millions of dollars have been raised for leukemia and lymphoma. The fact that struck me most powerfully as I watched purple shirted people struggle to the finish line was that these were not athletes in the conventional sense. Many were overweight, one was blind, another had a prosthetic leg and some were old. But each of them went the distance and could be seen around town that night and on subsequent days proudly wearing their Honolulu Marathon

### Marathon History

The distance of a Marathon is approximately the distance from the town of Marathon in Greece to Athens. In 490BC a Persian army landed on the Plain of Marathon with the intention of capturing Athens. A runner named Pheidippides was dispatched to Sparta to enlist the help of the Spartan army. He actually covered about 150 miles in 2 days, which is impressive. However, the Spartan army turned out not to be necessary because the Athenian army surprised the Persians, who were still in a preparation phase and, despite being outnumbered, the Athenians triumphed. A runner, not Pheidippides, was sent to Athens with news of the victory. Legend has it that he ran the 25 plus miles to Athens, delivered his message, "Rejoice we conquer.", and fell to the ground dead. Based on that story the marathon footrace was established.

The current distance of 26 miles, 385 yards (42.19k) was set in 1908 for the London Olympics so that the race would start at Windsor Castle and end in front of the Royal Box at Olympic Stadium in London. In 1926, this was adopted as the official distance of a marathon.

**Finishers** shirt.

The Leukemia and Lymphoma Society have trained tens of thousands of people to walk a marathon. They have proved to people over and over again that if you can walk one mile that, with training, you can walk 26 miles (42k) and earn the right to call yourself a marathoner.

### Training to Walk a Marathon

Take your time, there's no way that you can hurry up your readiness for a marathon, any more than a farmer can hurry up the growth of his crop if he doesn't plant the seeds in time. Teach yourself about pacing, so that you can find a speed that allows you to go the distance. This will be what they call aerobic walking where the oxygen that you breathe in matches the oxygen being used by the muscles involved in walking and posture. Learn to use your arms. They should be bent at the elbow and piston back and forth, not swinging across your body, which will give some unnecessary twist to the torso. (This is sometimes called *Rocking the baby*.) Gradually increase your distance week by week. Don't over train by walking hard every day. It's a good idea to look for some variety or cross training. This might be anything from swimming to Pilates, yoga to strength training, or a fitness class at the *YM/YWCA* or Curves.

Test your growing endurance by entering some local races such as a 5k and a 10k. This will give you the feel of the atmosphere of a race, and teach you what sort of pace you go when the adrenaline is flowing. It's a good idea to complete a half marathon before entering a full marathon. It's a learning experience to feel what it takes to walk 13 miles (21km) and will give you some feedback as to your readiness to go twice that distance.

If you are overweight, or heavier than you'd like to be, include some caloric restriction into your training program. A loss of 10, 15 or 20lbs (4.5, 7 or 9kg) makes a tremendous difference to your ability to walk the 26-plus miles (42k) without distress.

Stretch out your muscles after every workout and be prepared to stop and stretch during a long walk if you feel yourself getting stiff and sore. If a muscle feels really tight after a hard walk remember that ice and elevation

### Marathon Man

By Martin Collis

A tongue in cheek tribute to my old friend, George Sheehan, who died of cancer some years back. His influence on my thinking is reflected by the number of Sheehan quotes in this book.

George and Martin

I'm a marathon man
I'm a marathon man
I've got 26 pairs of shoes
I get high on the miles
I get high on the pain
And I don't need the drugs
and the booze
I've got shin splints
I've got athlete's foot
And my tendonitis glows
I've got bone spurs
I've got jock itch
My bursitis it comes and it goes
I'm a marathon man
I'm a marathon man

Chondromalacia is eating up my
knees
I called my daughter Gatorade
And my son Pheidippides
I've got a closet full of T-shirts
From every race that I ran
I glycogen loaded
Till my muscles exploded
'Cause I'm just a marathon man
I'm a marathon man
I'm a marathon man.

I went to Honolulu
And I ran up the Diamond Head
The Hawaiian sun
It got me on the run
But it's better to be red than
dead
I'm dehydrated and heat
prostrated
Drinking Gatorade by the can
An isotonic imbiber
For my slow twitch fibers
I'm just a marathon man
I'm a marathon man

I was running down in Boston
When I finally hit the wall
I died with my Nikes on my feet
It was a wonderful way to fall
I jogged up to the Pearly Gates
I heard an Angel chorus swell
Saying , "Come on in,
Little Marathon Man
You've had enough of hell.
You're a marathon man."

will speed its recovery.

Most things go better with a partner or a group and walking's no exception. Commitment to another person or group and a designated time increases the likelihood that your training will be successful.

Always be concerned about hydration, and on a long walk be prepared to refuel yourself with one of the many sports drinks or energy drinks, which are available.

Of course, there is a lot of information on the web and a good place to start is the Leukemia and Lymphoma Society Team-in-Training site, which has lots of information about the practicalities of marathon training and participation. More complete training information can be found at The Walking Site – Marathon Training (www.marathonwalking.com/training.html) Many people use power walking to improve their time when walking a marathon. For information on power walking and the excellent WoW Power Walking website see the last segment in Chapter 13 – *Walking With A Difference*.

### Walking a Cumulative Marathon

You are in charge of your walking program and you can set any goal you want. One interesting technique is to see how many days it takes you to walk the 26 miles 385 yards (42.19km) of a marathon. If you cover 1 mile a day it will clearly take you 26 days. The easy way to estimate this when using a pedometer is to say there are 2000 steps per mile (1250 steps per kilometer), which means that you will have to walk 52,737 steps to complete your marathon. You can increase your accuracy by measuring your average step length and dividing it into the marathon distance.

A way to increase your walking mileage is to gradually decrease the time it takes you to walk a marathon, and see how many marathons a month you can complete.

A further variation is to count only the continuous steps you do on a purposeful walk towards your *marathon* total. Any stimulus that gets you walking is a good one.

*This is the true joy in life, the being used for a purpose recognized by yourself as a mighty one: The being thoroughly worn out before you die: Being a force of nature instead of a feverish selfish little clod of ailments and grievances complaining that the world will not devote itself to making you happy.*

G. B. Shaw

# 13

# Walking With a Difference

### Pole Walking

Pole walking, or Nordic walking as it's often called, is rather like cross-country skiing without the snow. The reasons for pole walking's increasing popularity can be summarized as follows:

1. It's easy to learn.
2. It can provide some protection and relief for people with knee pain.
3. It burns more calories than normal walking without poles.
4. It is a workout for the upper body as well as the legs.
5. For older people, or others with balance problems, it offers stability.
6. It's affordable.

Pole walking got its start in Finland in the 1930's as a form of summer training for cross-country skiers and for many years that's where it stayed. But in the late 1990s some sort of 'tipping point' was passed and a regional activity suddenly spread throughout Europe. In Germany, the number of Nordic walkers went from 10,000 to 120,000 in the space of one year and two years further on, in 2004, the number had risen to 2.2 million. With multiple millions of pole walking adherents in Europe it was inevitable that

**Tombstones and Plaques**

### The Hyphen

*I read of a man who was asked to speak at the funeral of a friend.*
*He referred to the dates on the tombstone, the beginning and the end.*
*The first and the last days are markers in time. But what do those really mean?*
*What matters is not the birth or the death but the hyphen which lies in between.*

*For the hyphen is the time you spend on this earth, just a hyphen to show what a life's really worth.*
*And it isn't a house, it isn't a car, and it isn't a '53 Gibson guitar.*
*It's not a position, it's not a possession or membership in a prestigious profession.*
*It's not in the labels on your clothes or your shoes or the places you've been or seen on a cruise.*

*The words on the tombstones are kindness, and love, family, friendship and laughter.*
*These are the things that continue to ring when your body has reached the hereafter.*
*Choose wisely and well when selecting the goals that you choose to base your life on.*
*To miss the joy is to miss it all and a terrible waste of a hyphen.*

I once read a poem called "The Hyphen". I remembered some of the lines and I liked the concept. I restructured the poem using bits of the original and a lot of my own lines. I'd be delighted to acknowledge the original author in future editions of my book, if I can find out who it is.

Martin Collis

the activity would cross the Atlantic to North America.

Some major studies validated the claims that pole walking had more benefits the pole-less walking. Dr. Tim Church at the Cooper Institute found that pole walkers burned an average of 20% more calories when using poles, but that they perceived pole walking as no more strenuous than regular walking. Research at Finland's Helsinki Polytechnic showed that pole walking improved blood circulation and mobility of the neck and shoulder area, strengthened a variety of muscles in the upper body and, of course, increased cardiovascular fitness.

It's clear that one way to enhance your walking experience is to buy a pair of lightweight, rubber tipped, aluminum poles. The technique is to stand tall, with chest open and the bottom tucked in. The arms should be bent at about 90° and pumped back and forth like pistons as you stride along. You might look a little strange at WalMart, but certainly not out of place at Ikea.

### 5 Tips to Start Off With Good Form

1. Most poles are telescopic and can be adjusted to an appropriate length for your height. Make sure both poles are an identical length.
2. Start with your arms at your sides, letting the poles drag behind you. Gradually introduce a natural arm swing.
3. Keeping the leading arm fairly straight, bring it up to chest height. As the arm lowers, let the tip of the pole land lightly. With good technique it should land beside your opposite heel.
4. Still with the arm quite straight, push down through the pole to move the body forward.
5. Unlike cross-country skiing, the arms stay quite straight during pole walking.

### Elliptical Trainers

I have always been drawn to the idea of a low impact, physically challenging machine, which enables you to use both the muscles of the upper and lower body. In some ways I feel like the soft drink researcher who created 4-Up, 5-Up and 6-Up but never hit the jackpot of 7-Up. In the late 70s I worked with an old inventor, Mr. Tom Gibbs, to create a

Dr. Martin Collis testing a prototype of the original *Dynotron*

machine, which I named the *Dynotron*. It was essentially an elliptical trainer, except that we used a metal frame to allow the arms to assist the rotational movement. I was able to record very high oxygen uptakes and calorie burning on the *Dynotron*, which were similar to those of cross-country skiers. Prototypes were built, and factory space rented in Alberta, but our expertise was in equipment design, not business and somehow as new partners came onboard the money evaporated and many years went by before elliptical machines, as we now know them, became a feature in fitness facilities and home gyms.

The major advantage of modern elliptical machines is that they enable you to burn calories like a jogger, with minimal impact on the knees, hips, back and ankles. A moderate workout on an elliptical machine burns 12 to 13 calories per minute, compared with 5 calories per minute for someone walking at 3mph. Another benefit of an elliptical machine is that you can go in the reverse direction and go backwards on the pedals or platforms. This provides a balanced development for the musculature of the legs.

If you choose to buy an elliptical machine do some homework and try out various models in fitness clubs or in the store. Whether you're buying a pedometer, treadmill or elliptical trainer it's a good rule of thumb to avoid the very cheapest items. However, having said that, you can still acquire a reliable elliptical trainer for under $1000.

Ten features to consider in selecting your home use elliptical:
1. Make sure you have a full stride length of 21".
2. Upper arm handles are a must so that you can do a combined upper body and lower body workout.
3. At home, the 'quiet factor' is important, particularly if you want to watch a DVD or TV, or listen to music while you workout.
4. Check the warranty. A good machine should give you one year's parts and labor and up to 3 years for parts.
5. Personally, I like an LCD display, which clearly shows things like time, calories, heart rate and other information and offers a variety of pre-set programs.
6. The pedals should have a textured 'non-slip' surface and a curved lip to prevent the possibility of the feet slipping off the pedal while exercising.

Write down 5 things that you love to do and date when you last did them.

1.

2.

3.

4.

5.

It's not uncommon to find busy people who have not done one of their five favorite activities in over a year.

Carpe diem.

7. A small luxury feature, which I like, is a built-in fan, which makes your workout more comfortable.

8. Rear drive or front drive? This refers to the placement of the flywheel at the front or back of the elliptical trainer. Most consumer reports prefer the rear driven elliptical, which tends to be more expensive but offers a smoother, more natural motion. If you select a front drive machine make sure it features articulating pedals to keep the ride smooth.

9. One of the big differences between cheap and more expensive machines is whether they use steel or plastic for most of their construction.

10. A feature I find useful and convenient is the ability to save a sequence you have just used so that you can repeat it subsequently. In other words, you can customize and save your workouts.

**Note:** I find that my pedometer records every 'step' that I do on my elliptical machine. If your own pedometer tends to miss some 'steps' on your elliptical workout, you will find that most machines display calories burned, which you can multiply by 20 to approximate your step count.

Lastly, you don't have to buy a new machine. Fitness equipment can often be found in newspaper advertisements and second-hand stores. I will remind you to make sure you have sufficient space. Elliptical trainers take up quite a bit of space and they aren't pretty, so you need a home gym or basement where it won't look out of place.

### Treadmills

At first glance, a treadmill looks like a metaphor for the stressed suburbanite; walking, jogging, sweating and getting nowhere. Images of hamsters endlessly spinning on their wheels come to mind. But for many people treadmills provide a useful solution to achieve walking or jogging goals when weather, circumstances or safety keep them indoors. I've found that a good treadmill workout is anything but boring. Higher end treadmills offer a variety of programs, which will have you changing speed, incline and intensity. A set of headphones or speakers can provide your favorite tunes to energize you and a DVD can have you on a virtual walk through the greatest scenery in the world. The Journal of the American Medicine Association reported a study in which people with home

*We wish to acknowledge the magazine 'Stitches',
a Canadian journal of medical humor,
for many of our cartoons.*

"I usually do two hours of cardio and then four
more of cardio and then two more of cardio."

treadmills were more successful at losing weight on a walking program than subjects with no treadmill.

The usual caveats about purchasing home fitness equipment are particularly relevant to treadmills because of their size. Before you buy, make sure to have a number of treadmill walks at a local gym or recreation centre. Like an elliptical trainer, a treadmill is not a pretty piece of furniture and will need space in a recreation room, basement or home gym. Because a number of people buy treadmills and get little use out of them there are always bargains to be found online, in second hand equipment stores and newspaper classified advertisements. Lastly, if you've convinced yourself that you're going to use a home treadmill regularly, get a good one.

### Guidelines for Treadmill Selection

1.  Get a motorized treadmill. The non-motorized treadmills often have you walking with an unnatural gait. It's sometimes hard to get the belt moving on a non-motorized machine and you will be unable to change the incline during a workout, without dismounting and starting over.
2.  The heart of your treadmill is the motor so you want one with power. Knowing a little terminology will help you from being misled. The horsepower figure you want to look at is "continuous duty rating" and this should be at least 1 1/2 HP to 2 1/2 HP. Be careful of terms like ""peak duty" and "treadmill duty", which are less useful. Look for at least a one-year warranty on a new machine.
3.  The machine should have the ability to vary the incline, so that you are walking uphill. Look for an incline range of at least 10%.
4.  You cannot walk much faster than 4mph (6.4kmh) but I suggest a machine that will go up to 10mph so that you have room to jog and the machine is not running close to its maximum speed.
5.  The bed, or belt, should provide plenty of room so that you don't feel concerned about stepping off the side or the back of the treadmill. I like the belt to be around 50" (125cm) long and at least 18" (45cm) wide.
6.  The bed should have some resilience so that it's comfortable to walk on. Big, solid rollers tend to produce a smoother walk, which means less impact on your joints.
7.  Look for a quiet machine. It's easier to listen to music or watch

*Me thinks that the moment my legs begin to move, my thoughts begin to flow.*

Henry D. Thoreau

*Happy the person who has acquired a love of walking for its own sake.*

W. J. Holland

TV and it doesn't disturb everybody else in the house. As a general rule, better-constructed machines make less noise and DC motors tend to run most quietly.

8. Make sure the machine is stable. Some lighter machines tend to wobble, which is noisy and bad for you and the treadmill. Safety rails on either side of the moving bed need to be close enough to grab onto easily and yet not too close so as to interfere with your arm motion. The handrails should be sturdy enough to support your weight if you wish to lift your feet from the bed. Another useful safety feature is a magnet, which is attached from a lead on your body to the consol on the treadmill. If the contact is broken, the treadmill immediately stops.

9. I like a clear LCD display on the treadmill consol. Most treadmills will provide basic information such as time, distance, calories, gradient and speed. Many people like to monitor their heart rate, which can be done on some models by wireless telemetry or on most by gripping contacts, which count your pulse. Look for interesting pre-set programs and interactive features, which allow you to build your own program. Personally, I can do without the motivational slogans that show up on some displays.

10. Treadmills are great for step counting with your pedometer. Unlike an exercise cycle, your pedometer shouldn't miss a step as you walk or jog on the endless belt.

A website which is a useful resource for all forms of exercise and equipment is www.about.com. Just type in the exercise equipment you are researching in their 'search' feature to bring up a list of articles.

### Steppers

Stepping machines come in many different forms, sizes and prices. There are tread steppers, stair climbers, lateral thigh steppers and lots more. One, which I have found very useful, is the little mini-stepper, which I have in my TV room. It has two non-slip foot pedals on hydraulic shocks and keeps track of my time, number of steps and calories burned. Working against the

*I was the world in which I walked.*

Wallace Stevens

*The best effect of any book is that it
excites the reader to self-activity.*

Thomas Carlyle

resistance of the shocks tones the quads and the glutes and delivers a good cardio workout. I use mine to do some step counting during TV commercials or while watching a show.

Many mini-steppers come with elastic tubing so that you can work the arms simultaneously with the legs. The mini-stepper is a useful little device, which is inexpensive and takes up little room, but can help turn a TV room or other area into a calorie burning gym.

### Walking in Water

Walking on water is tricky and can only be accomplished by people to whom the laws of physics do not apply. However, walking, or jogging, in water is an accepted way to work the leg muscles with minimal impact on the joints and ligaments. Because of this it's a favorite method for injury rehabilitation and can also be used by walkers who have problems such as blisters, ingrown toenails, shin splints and other conditions that might be aggravated by regular walking.

In years gone by the activity was referred to as 'treading water', which is an apt description, but now you're more likely to see it called 'pool running', 'deep water jogging' or 'aqua fitness'. Because of the natural resistance of the water this activity is a good leg workout and cardiovascular stimulus. The motion tends to be a high knee jogging motion more than the normal walking pattern. The arms can be brought into play to help with flotation and provide some exercise for the upper body.

Deep water jogging can be performed with or without a floatation belt. The floatation belt will keep you higher in the water and enables you to focus on getting a good leg workout. Personally I prefer to work without the belt using my arms and legs to keep my head comfortably above water.

This is a terrific workout and is used by high-level athletes and even racehorses to rehabilitate injury, I find that I get about 50+ leg cycles (100 *steps*) per minute, so that 10 minutes of pool running will give me 1,000

*A twist inward*
*A transformation outward*
*A fresh view from fatigued eyes*
*All part of a simple design*
*Of much complexity*
*With the whole greater*
*Than the sum of the steps*
*All the while traveling*
*One step at a time.*

From Suzanne Moody's poem
'The Labyrinth'

*steps*. Because of the intensity of the work caused by the resistance of the water, I double the *value* of the *steps* that I do in the water. If I wanted to record my steps, my 10- minutes of pool running would be 2,000 steps. Just think in terms of 1,000 *steps* every 5 minutes, and don't try to go too long at first, as it's tiring.

Most public pools run classes in pool running where you can learn a variety of ways to maximize the benefits of this form of aquatic exercise.

### The Labyrinth – A Walking Meditation

The labyrinth can be seen as a metaphor for our journey through life. Labyrinths in one form or another have been with us for over 4,000 years and are a feature of many cultures. You don't walk a labyrinth to get physically fit, so you can let go of step counting, burning calories and other physical aspects of walking. Labyrinths are about spiritual fitness and combine the imagery of the circle and the spiral into a meandering but purposeful path. The labyrinth as we know it today is not a maze. A maze is a puzzle with many ways to go wrong. A labyrinth has but one path; there are no blind alleys. Following the circuitous path will lead you to the center and out again.

The first time I saw people walking a labyrinth was at Grace Cathedral in San Francisco and I picked up a pamphlet to find out what these quiet focused walkers were doing. The pamphlet spoke of the "threefold path".

1. **Releasing**. At the start of the labyrinth try to release, or let go of, everyday worries and concerns.
2. **Receiving**. When you get to the center, open yourself up to receive the wisdom of the universe. It's at the center you look for illumination, insight and focus.
3. **Integrating**. The path out is where you take ownership of the thoughts that have come to you. On the outward path many people feel empowered and energized as they return to the world outside the labyrinth.

You can achieve a labyrinth-like feeling on any walk, particularly if its one you walk on a regular basis. You can choose an inward walk where you clear your mind and allow the universe to enter. You can focus on the

*To find new things, take the path
you took yesterday.*

John Burroughs

*If you are seeking creative ideas,
go out walking.*

Raymond Inmon

things around you including the sky, the trees and flowers or the other people on your path. Every few walks it's worth just noticing the miracle of your own breath, taking in oxygen, which journeys through the lungs and onto hemoglobin in the blood where it's transported throughout the body, but particularly to the big muscles in the legs, that without oxygen would cease to function.

Some people are healed by the laying on of hands; labyrinth walkers find healing in the laying on of feet.

If you need more information about labyrinths there are many websites devoted to the topic.

### Cobblestone Walking

The Chinese have used 'stone stepping' or cobblestone walking for centuries. Essentially it is a do-it-yourself form of foot reflexology. (If you are unfamiliar with foot reflexology, it is a method of activating the acupoints in the feet, which in turn stimulate various organs and systems in the body.) Anecdotal evidence from China has reported that regular cobblestone walking, which is more typically practiced by older adults, is associated with lowered blood pressure, decreased sensations of pain, better balance and a generally improved quality of life. The number of specially laid out cobblestone walks in China and their continued use suggested that there were real benefits to this form of activity, but these benefits had not been documented by scientific study.

Dr. John Fisher of the Oregon Research Institute, after visiting China, decided to research the practice. He stated, *We visited China and noticed that numerous adults spent 30 minutes each day walking, standing and sometimes dancing on these beautifully laid cobblestone paths. They did this for their health every day of the week. For our study, we used manufactured mats that replicated these cobblestone paths.*

In a pilot study, the scientists divided the 48 older adult participants into a control group, who did regular walking and social activities, and an experimental group, who used the cobblestone mats. Each group did three 45 minutes sessions a week. The results were impressive. The cobblestone walkers reported significant improvement in performing the activities of daily living (ADL), better sleep, decreased perception of pain and

*Good resolutions are like babies crying
in church or at a concert; they should
be carried out immediately.*

Charles M. Sheldon

*Habituate yourself to walk far.*

Thomas Jefferson

significant measured decreases in resting diastolic blood pressure. The study was published in the Journal of Aging and Physical Activity and Dr. Fisher and his colleague Dr. Fuzhong Li have received funding from the National Institute of Aging to continue their research.

This is an intriguing variation on day to day walking and has the advantage of being an indoor activity, which could make it a good foul weather alternative. Various dealers now carry cobblestone mats, which can be found with ease on the web.

### Power Walking

The main difference between power walking and regular walking is speed and intensity. Power walking begins somewhere over 4 miles per hour (6.4k per hour) and can go as high as 7 miles per hour (11.2k per hour), which is faster than most people jog. If people tell you that walking's not enough to really impact your fitness level, take them on a power walk and let them puff and sweat and feel what it's like to sustain a stepping speed of around 150 steps a minute.

Good technique and posture are always important, but never more so than in power walking. Power walking tips include:

(I)  Don't try to take bigger steps. Increase your stepping cadence so that you are doing more steps each minute.

(II)  Walk tall. Imagine the top of the head being pulled up by an invisible string. Your eyes should be looking forward, not downwards. (If you keep finding old lottery tickets and spare change on your walk it's a sign that your head and eyes are downcast.) Remember the old song, "All our eyes on, the distance horizon" and keep your eyes focused ahead. If you need to look down, use your eyes, not your head.

(III)  Avoid the old 'chin up, chest out' instruction, but keep the shoulders down and back and relaxed. This will naturally bring the chest up.

(IV)  Keep a solid stack of vertebrae with your spine aligned and straight.

(V)  Use your arms, with elbows bent at about 90° and in a short compact swing. Always keep the arms in the same plain going forward and back, never swinging across your body.

(VI)  The heel-sole-toe roll is important. Think of having springs in your calf muscles and your toes that will power you into the next step.

*As you think, so shall you be.*

This is part of the thinking
of most major religions.

*Hope is the thing with feathers*
*That perches on the soul*
*And sings the song*
*Without the words*
*And never stops at all.*

Emily Dickinson

*I'll tell you how to reach the highest high*
*You'll laugh and say, "Nothing is that simple."*

Pete Townshend

Roll through the full length of your foot and not only show someone behind you a 'clean pair of heels' but also the soles of your shoes as you launch yourself off your toes and into the next step.

(VII) Breathe naturally, rhythmically and deeply to supply the working, walking muscles with plenty of oxygen. Walking aerobically means that you are taking in enough oxygen to match the oxygen that you are using, so that you might be breathing hard, but will not be 'out of breath'.

(VIII) One of the great benefits of power walking is that you can get all the cardiovascular and fitness benefits of jogging with a lot less likelihood of injury. Compared to slower walking, power walking will reward you with more steps in less time, greater physiological benefits and an awareness that you are still an athlete as you push pace up to the limits of your ability. With dedication and training many people power walk marathons in less than 6 hours.

There is a wonderful website titled WoW Power Walking [www.wowpowerwalking.com]. It features a walking events calendar, training schedules, results, news, corporate programs, FAQs and newsletters. My two favorite sections on WoW are *Walkers Talking* and for inspiration, *Success Stories*, which include photographs and information and gives you the feeling of really being an insider in the power walking community.

*Be your own hero, it's cheaper than a movie ticket.*

Doug Horton

*How you think when you lose determines
how long it will be before you win.*

G. K. Chesterton

*If you find a path with no obstacles,
check and see if it leads anywhere.*

Alan Joseph

# 14

# Life Change

### Be Your Own Hero

Much of this book is about practical things, such as walking more and eating better and making changes in your life to create a fitter, slimmer, happier you. The changes and lifestyle I suggest would be easier to do if you didn't live in a society that has engineered physical activity out of your daily life and that surrounds you with cheap food and drink at every turn. If you go with the cultural flow it is very, very probable that you will become sedentary and overweight. Remember, you live in a culture that has soft drink machines in funeral parlors; food at gas stations and celebrates every occasion from Fridays, to promotions to Christmas with thousands of calories. You need to be a bit of a hero to fight against the cultural tide of consumption. It's a wonderful feeling to make a promise to yourself and keep it and know you're not a puppet of the multinational marketers.

Change does not come easily and it's worth listening to the wisdom of others and to be inspired by heroes who overcame challenges far greater than turning down a beer or walking late in the evening to get 10,000 steps.

I find role models and heroes everywhere I turn. When I walk to my local store I invariably seem to see Penny Marsden, tiny, determined and

293

*Success rests in having the courage and endurance and, above all, the will to become the person you are, however peculiar that may be. Then you will be able to say, "I have found my hero and it is me."*

George Sheehan

*I was once accused of being, 'a legend in my own mind.' Of course I am, and you should be too. Each one of us must be a hero. We are here to lead a heroic life. When we cease to lead such lives, we no longer truly exist.*

George Sheehan

pushing her walker as though her life depended on it, which it probably does. (Maybe the expression should be, *as if her **quality** of life depended on it,* which it certainly does). Until a short while ago she always walked with her husband George, who died at age 95. George not only kept his body in shape by walking, but also kept his mind alive by auditing courses at the University of Victoria. [Read more about George and Penny at: http://www.speakwell.com/well/2003fall/visions.shtml] Then there's Mavis Lundgren, who completed her first marathon aged 70 and when last seen was competing in her $62^{nd}$ marathon, aged 92 in Portland. [http://www.speakwell.com/well/2002_spring/4.shtml]

Elsewhere in the book I mentioned that TOO is often used as a blocking word and is an acronym for Totally Out Of the question as in, *I'm too old, too uncoordinated, too embarrassed, too heavy, too busy* and many more. In a song titled, *It's Never Too Late*, I wrote:

*It's never too late to be what you might have been*
*And it's never too late to see what you might have seen*
*You have the magic to wipe clean the slate*
*It's never to late to say, "It's never too late."*

### Stepping Out of Your Comfort Zone

In order to change, to grow, and to improve you will have to make changes in your life. Remember, if you do what you've always done, you'll be what you've always been or, put another way; doing the same thing over and over again and expecting a different result is a form of insanity. So if you start on a new venture or program and find yourself in a setting that is uncomfortable and challenging there's a good chance of some growth and change occurring. I'll give a personal example. In my early 60s, after narrowly dodging death in a car accident, I decided to put my uninjured body to good use and compete in my first triathlon. I trained hard and felt I was ready. However, I was unprepared for the mayhem at the start of the swim. People kicked me, swam over the top of me, knocked off my goggles and generally made life uncomfortable. I remember the thoughts going through my mind, *This is ridiculous. I don't need to do this. I don't belong here. Is this some kind of delayed mid-life crisis?* But I kept going and about 1/2 an hour later stumbled out of the lake slightly ahead of my schedule. I forgot which row my bike was in, but that's another story. Despite that initial

*Failure is the condiment that gives success its flavor.*

Truman Capote

*Life is what we make it, always has been, always will be.*

Grandma Moses

*An overweight, unhealthy, disheveled and unemployed man looks at a contemporary who is power walking and apparently full of energy and successful. He has one thought, "There but for me goes I."*

Unknown

discomfort, I came to really enjoy triathlons and completing that first one was one of the highlights of my year.

If you show up to new situations or challenges with a positive attitude, some form of success is inevitable because even *failure* becomes a learning experience. Failure is just an acronym for, *Found Another Important Lesson Upon Receiving Experience* or, as Thomas Beckett said:

> *Try again,*
> *Fail again,*
> *Fail better.*

Sir Winston Churchill put it all in perspective when he said:

> *Success is not final*
> *Failure is not fatal*
> *It's the courage to continue that counts.*

We humans are a remarkable species, there's Beethoven who was sickly and stone deaf and yet wrote some of the greatest classical music ever written and Jean-Dominique Bauby who was totally paralyzed except for his left eyelid in what is called 'locked in syndrome', but who developed a code by blinking his eyelid; letters became words, words became sentences and sentences gave birth to his book, *The Diving Bell and the Butterfly*. Then there are the athletes such as Terry Fox, hop-skipping over a marathon a day in his effort to be the first amputee to *run* across Canada and Rick Hansen who propelled his wheelchair around the world, not in 80 days, but in 2 years, 2 months and 2 days. Lance Armstrong not only overcame testicular cancer, which spread to his gut, lungs and brain, but took his cancer ravaged body/mind and trained it to such a level that he became the greatest cyclist in the history of the Tour de France, the toughest bike ride in the world. (See Summer 'Well' 2005 for the article 'Terry, Dick, Rick and Lance',
http://www.speakwell.com/well/2005summer/excellerators.php)

What's your excuse? *I'm tired; I don't have time; it's my metabolism.* None of them stand up. We are all human and we can all rise to a challenge, we all have the capacity for greatness within us. What gets in the way are things

### Guru du Jour

Music and lyrics by Martin Collis

Tired and weary
Broken and blue
Too much theory
I need a guru

To help me lose weight
To help with my stress
They're on the Internet
They're on P.B.S.

If the Guru du Jour
Just isn't for you
Head to the bookstore
For a g'nother Guru.

I've been Andrew Weil'd
I've been Oprah'd
Steven Coveyed
Deepak Chopra'd

And just when I think
I've got it all wrong
Antony Robbins
Comes bob-bob-bobbin' along

I've been Susan Powtered
On every diet
Atkins to the Zone
They write it I'll buy it

I've been Richard Simmons'd
Is it her or him?
My body is fat
My wallet is thin

Just when I think
My fat cells are wrong
Antony Robbins
Comes bob-bob-bobbin'
along.

There's only one Guru
That can help you win
It's walking around
Inside your skin

You are the trainer
The dietician is you
You're the psychologist
You're the Guru

such as self-pity and feeling like a victim. As Oliver Wilson once said, *What poison is to food, self-pity is to life.* When we allow the worst of us to get the best of us we are failing to come close to our human potential. The singer Eliza Gilkyson expressed this sentiment well in a recent song when she said, *You let the little dreams live and the big ones die.*

We have become so used to comfort, convenience stores, instant entertainment and pharmaceutical fixes that we have lost sight of our personal potential. We are blind to the paradox that indulging ourselves in comfort and convenience leads to a life of discomfort and inconvenience as the body rebels against a poor diet and lack of movement. The true self-indulgence lies in regular physical activity and nutritious food. The active life is the one that gives you permission to be all that you can be. In the words of the great writer, philosopher and walker, William James, *The strenuous life tastes better.*

Everybody who tells me that they *don't have time to exercise* misses the point. People who exercise regularly have more time, because, although physical activity uses energy it creates more, and your life runs on energy. Without energy we do things badly or not at all. The 24 hours we are given start to shrink because we lack the stamina to use them. Your daily walk, your time at the gym isn't stealing an hour from your day, it's helping create a vibrant person who will have more hours for work, play and family.

Ringo Starr told us, *You know it don't come easy* and he might well have been talking about lifestyle change. Sedentary habits die hard and the overworked chemistry of your body might have become adjusted to your habit of eating until you're stuffed rather than satisfied. Samuel Johnson warned us that, *The chains of habit can be too small to be felt until they are too strong to be broken.* So be prepared for some hand-to-hand combat with yourself and society if you are going to lose weight or move from a sedentary to an active life. But remember, once you get them, good habits are also hard to break. This book is designed to provide you with solid information and plenty of motivation and this will get you started, but it's habits that will get you where you need to go.

In the end, it's not philosophers, psychologists, scientists, writers, doctors or personal trainers who will be responsible for you moving

*Nothing can stop the person with the right mental attitude from achieving their goal; nothing on earth can help the person with the wrong mental attitude.*

Thomas Jefferson

*There is no planet, sun or star could hold you if you but knew what you are.*

Ralph Waldo Emerson

*There are no shortcuts to anyplace worth going.*

Beverly Sills

towards a better life. It's you keeping your promises to yourself day after day after day. The homespun wisdom of Roger Miller put it this way.

*All you gotta do, is put your mind to it
Knuckle down, buckle down and do it, do it, do it.*

As Sir Winston Churchill thundered to the students at Harrow School.

*Never give in. Never give in.
Never, never, never, never, never give in.*

That's how heroes are made.

*Take what you can gather from coincidence.*

Bob Dylan

*What lies beyond us and what lies before us are tiny matters when compared to what lies within us.*

Ralph Waldo Emerson

*There is only one journey. Going inside yourself.*

Rainer Maria Rilke

# 15

# The Power of Fifteen

### Introduction

Sometimes the cosmic tumblers fall into place, which is what appeared to happen with the *Power of Fifteen*. I knew that in order to lose weight most people have to eat less and move more. I experimented with the calorie intake/calorie expenditure formula and found that about 1500 quality calories and 15,000 daily steps produced a steady weekly weight loss of 3 to 4 lbs. (1.3 to 1.8kg) and feelings of increased energy and health.

To maintain overall mind/body function I turned to the Sun Salutation and found that from Mountain pose to Mountain pose (beginning to completion) was 15 moves. The Power of Fifteen was completed by the peaceful, mind altering 15 controlled 15-second breaths.

I've been told that coincidence is some sort of celestial pun, or maybe God's way of remaining anonymous, but as I laid out the book with the Power of Fifteen as the closing chapter, I was delighted, but not really surprised, to find that it was Chapter 15.

### Healthy Weight Loss and Weight Maintenance

It's difficult to see through the half-truths, deceptions, false promises, small print and outright lies of people and promotions telling you that

*If people around you aren't going anywhere, if their dreams are no bigger than hanging out on the corner, or if they're dragging you down, get rid of them. Negative people can sap your energy so fast, and they can take your dreams from you, too.*

Earvin 'Magic' Johnson

*Anything less than a conscious commitment to the important is an unconscious commitment to the unimportant.*

Stephen Covey

losing weight will be easy and that they can transform your body in only minutes each week. The country singer Jimmie Dale Gilmour wrote about the "half truths that are always half lies" and another singer, Tom Waits told us that *the big print giveth and the small print taketh away.*

I feel we do people a tremendous disservice when we misrepresent a product or program in order too make a sale. We also short change people by failing to challenge them and assuming that North Americans are 'soft'. I believe that we are all athletes, some of us in training and some of us not, but we all have potential. We're Canadians not Can'tadians, we're Americans not American'ts.

This chapter is not for the faint hearted or those looking for a quick fix. This if for readers who want to lose weight and get into great shape, maybe the best shape of their lives. This is for people looking for a breakthrough.

The number '15' has always resonated with me, it's known as *the magic constant* in one branch of mathematics. Jamie Oliver's breakthrough London restaurant is called *Fifteen*, there are fifteen psalms in the *Songs of Ascent* and, of course, everybody feels entitled to their *15 minutes of fame*.

## My Personal Experience

I came to The Power of Fifteen through observation and experimentation. Coincidentally, I wanted to lose about 15lbs (7kg) and walking 12,000 steps a day wasn't doing it. A big part of the answer clearly lay in caloric restriction and, as I wrote in The Great Diet Debate ('Well' Fall 2002, www.speakwell.com/well/2002_fall/1a.shtml), if you follow many of the big name diets, be they low fat, low carb, high protein, vegetarian or fat/carb/protein ratios, you finish up consuming just under 1600 calories a day. But, as I noted earlier in the book, weight loss without exercise is not ideal, as the body tends to metabolize muscle as well as fat. So the best chance of long term weight loss and weight control comes from a combination of physical activity, which protects muscles from being metabolized by the body, and caloric restriction.

My formula was simple. Increase my steps to 15,000 a day and decrease my calories to 1500 a day. 15 X 15 was what it took for quick, manageable

*Sometimes your best is not enough, you have to do what's required.*

Winston Churchill

*It's easier to make big changes in diet than moderate ones – if you know what changes to make.*

Dean Ornish, MD

and inevitable weight loss. The 15,000 steps are important for cardiovascular health and long-term maintenance, but it's the 1500 calories that hold the key to weight loss. After losing 10lbs (4.5kg) in 2 weeks I relaxed and went to a number of social meals and ate carelessly, and found that the daily weight loss stopped. It was a short, sharp reminder that caloric control is the key to weight loss, while physical activity is the key to overall health and weight maintenance.

### Weight Loss

### 15,000 Steps

Fifteen thousand steps a day is not for everybody, because it takes time. A one-hour walk will give you about half your total, and an active day will take care of another five thousand steps. This still leaves about three thousand steps, which are relatively easy to find. The key is the one major walk each day. If 15,000 steps is unrealistic, move towards it, find excuses and reasons to walk, knowing that each extra step is in the direction of health, weight control and well being. Like any substantial challenge, it's usually a good idea to tackle it incrementally if you're not an habitual walker.

I believe that the key to getting to 15000 steps is an early morning walk. This sets you up for the day and gives you a lot of hours to add to your morning total. Get up early and go out on the street where you'll probably see cyclists, runners, joggers and walkers, who have figured out that aerobic exercise is a great way to start the day. Get off the train or bus a few stops early and walk to work. If you need to beat the traffic, drive to work early, park your car and then 'park' yourself. (i.e. find a nearby park for a walk). Where there's a will, there's a way and it's up to you to find it.

When you have reached your target weight and moved into a maintenance program, you might want to adjust your step count back towards 10,000, or you might find that walking has become a positive addiction that you wish to increase rather than decrease.

### 1500 Calories

Remember, 1500 calories is part of a weight **loss** regimen. Once you have achieved your target weight you can add to your daily calories until

*Reality check: you can never, ever, use weight loss to solve problems that are not related to your weight. At your goal weight or not, you still have to live with yourself and deal with your problems. You will still have the same husband, the same job, the same kids, the same life. Losing weight is not a cure for life.*

Phillip C. McGraw

*The Ultimate Weight Solution:*

*The 7 Keys to Weight Loss Freedom*, 2003

*I recently had my annual physical examination, which I get once every seven years, and when the nurse weighed me, I was shocked to discover how much stronger the Earth's gravitational pull has become since 1999.*

Dave Barry

*People say that losing weight is no walk in the park. When I hear that I think, yeah, that's the problem.*

Chris Adams

you are at a comfortable weight maintenance level.

I write about controlling caloric consumption in Chapter 6, *So You Really, Really Want to Lose Weight*, under the heading, *Losing It Yourself*. Fifteen hundred calories a day is plenty to provide you with all the nutrients you need and still leave room for a few favorite treats. You must have some clarity about how you're going to accomplish a fifteen hundred calorie lifestyle. It's a cliché, but people who fail to plan are really planning to fail. What you eat has to be your decision based on your fifteen hundred calorie limits, not on what other people around you are consuming. You can still celebrate, you can still be social, and you can still eat out without cramming in thousands of calories.

It's not easy to go it alone and you can sometimes increase your chances of success by joining an organization such as Weight Watchers or TOPS (Take Off Pounds Sensibly), which are inexpensive and will provide built-in social support and dietary ideas. If you need to lose a lot of weight, as I noted in Chapter 6, you might well benefit from a reputable hospital-based program in the US or a medically supervised program, such as the Dr. Bernstein Health and Diet Clinics in Canada and the US. If you are more than 80lbs (36kg) overweight, walking might be difficult at first, but as your weight comes down it's time for your steps to go up. One positive perspective on major weight loss is, that your legs will have been used to supporting a lot of weight. For example, legs that might have been pushing around 250lbs (113kg) will feel stronger and renewed when that weight goes down to 170lb (77kg).

There are various weight loss programs available in book form and on the Internet. You can choose to follow one of these precisely or use them for ideas about portion control, eating style and recipes. The dietary path you choose will have a lot to do with your personal preferences. I will list a few possibilities for you to consider, each of which will have its own set of advantages and drawbacks.

- **Eat like a diabetic**
  Both the American and Canadian Diabetes Associations have lots of guidance about losing weight while eating well.

*Make your goal out of reach but not out of sight.*

Anita de Franz

*Real glory springs from the
silent conquest of ourselves.*

Joseph Thompson

*If you have formed the habit of checking on every
new diet that comes along, you will find that,
mercifully, they all blur together, leaving you
with only one definite piece of information:
French-fried potatoes are out.*

Jean Kerr

- **Eat vegetarian**
  (I)   Dean Ornish, MD has an excellent book titled, *Eat More, Weigh Less*, which is well written, well referenced and contains recipes from some of North America's most celebrated chefs.
  (II)  John McDougall, MD has a number of books, which can be found on his website (www.drmcdougall.com), *The McDougall Plan for Maximum Weight Loss* is a reliable way to lose weight on a vegetarian diet. He also offers some residential courses, which could be a great way to kick-start a weight loss program.
- **Heart Healthy Eating, which includes meat and fish**
  (I)   *The Healthy Heart Cookbook* by Joe Piscatella.
        Joe Piscatella is not a physician but has produced a number of books, which are medically sound and easy to use. His passion for eating well and living well began at age 32, when he had a heart attack and realized he had to make some major lifestyle changes. He is an excellent speaker whose PBS produced DVD is both informative and inspiring.
  (II)  Heart and Stroke organizations in both the USA and Canada also have plenty of information about healthy eating styles that will help weight control.
- **Low Carb Weight Loss**
  (I)   The man who made low-carbohydrate diets famous, Dr. Atkins, is no longer with us, but his diet lives on. The diet is controversial, but many of the critics have not read Dr. Atkins' carefully constructed 4-phase diet in detail. Suffice it to say it's not all cheeseburgers and sausage and to quote directly from the book, *Dr. Atkins' New Diet Revolution. Exercise is non-negotiable. If you are not getting regular exercise, you aren't following the Atkins Nutritional Approach.* About vegetables, Atkins writes, *Let us sing a song of veggies, such beautiful, health enhancing, varied foods.* The Atkins approach might not be sustainable for as long as he claims, but it is an effective weight loss program that has worked for tens of thousands of people. For more details on Atkins and other diets go to The Great Diet Debate ('Well' Fall 2002, www.speakwell.com/well/2002_fall/1a.shtml)
  (II)  *The South Beach Diet* by Dr. Arthur Agatston
        This diet has a number of similarities to the Atkins diet with its structured phases and low carb emphasis. Dr. Agatston prefers

### It Doesn't All Add Up

I recently saw a book about walking and weight loss, which claimed that you'd lose 15lbs of fat in a 6-week walking based program, 'without dieting', according to the cover. I was intrigued and totaled the suggested step count for the 6 weeks. It added up to about 175,000, which, at approximately 20 steps per calorie, means you'd burn 8700 calories. With 3500 calories to a pound, you would burn off only 2 1/2lbs (1.1kg) of weight if you ate carefully. Needless to say the book was completely devoid of statistical support.

to talk in terms of *right carbs and right fats* instead of *low carbs and low fats*. If you follow the diet consistently you will lose weight quickly and safely. *The South Beach Diet* is available in book form and in a well-presented online program.

That's just a small sampling of the many approaches to weight loss that are currently available. As I noted earlier, any diet that keeps your calorie consumption around 1500 calories will lead to weight loss. There's no magic in any commercial diet, but you might find one that you like and that gives you the direction and motivation to take you to your weight loss goal.

A bigger challenge than losing weight, is maintaining it, and physical activity plays a major part in weight maintenance. Dr. James Hill, North America's leading researcher in weight maintenance says, *In fact, I'm beginning to think that weight loss is a different process than weight maintenance and it's the latter that is more important. Keeping it off has to do with how willing you are to change your life.* Hill is the co-director of the National Weight Loss Registry, which is following more that 3000 people who have lost an average of 60lbs (27kg) and kept it off for 5 years. There is a striking similarity about how these people maintain their weight loss.

1) **Regular physical activity** averaging over 400 calories a day. (400 calories would only be 8000 steps).
2) **Eat plenty of fruits and vegetables** (Complex carbohydrates).
3) **Eat breakfast**
4) **Weigh themselves frequently**

These people do not lose touch with their bodies or the possibility of weight gain. They commit themselves to a lifetime of healthy eating and exercise habits. As Dr. Susan Roberts of Tufts University says, *Most slim people can't eat everything they want, when they want it.* This is essentially the way of the world, sustained success in any area demands discipline, but the payoffs far outweigh the minor sacrifices. There's a fridge magnet that says, *Nothing tastes as good as slim feels.* It's hard to argue with a magnet.

*Sun salutations can energize and warm you, even on the darkest, coldest winter day.*

Carol Krucoff

*The yoga mat is a good place to turn to when therapy and antidepressants aren't enough.*

Amy Weintraub

# The Power of Fifteen – Part 2

### The Sun Salutation

*Fifteen flowing moves, which take you from Mountain to Mountain.*

The primary focus of this book is walking and weight control and the wellness that comes from them. Walking is wonderful, but it's one-dimensional and, in order to function in an optimal way and enhance your walking experiences, you need more. You need a sequence of moves that stimulates your limbs from head to toe and has a positive impact on your major organs.

The Sun Salutation is a yoga sequence that has been practiced for 5000 years. The word *yoga* comes from the same root as *yoke,* meaning connected or linked, and the Sun Salutation can be a link between the body and mind. If you were limited to one exercise this is the one.

- Weak areas are strengthened
- The circulation of blood and lymph is enhanced
- Body parts that tend to be compressed or contracted are stretched and opened
- Respiratory capacity is expanded
- Morning stiffness will be reduced or eliminated
- Weight bearing in the spine, hips and wrists can help prevent the onset of osteoarthritis and osteoporosis
- Every body part is involved from head to toes

*Mountain pose teaches us, literally, how to stand on our own two feet - teaching us to root ourselves into the earth. Our bodies become a connection between heaven and earth.*

Carol Krucoff

*Some people regard discipline as a chore, for me it sets me free to fly.*

Julie Andrews

*Hatha yoga teachers often say that if you do only one asana a day, make it a Sun Salutation. Sun Salutations are often incorporated into a yoga practice to limber up the whole body in preparation for other more difficult asanas. For people with limited time, the Sun Salutation is excellent because it stretches and strengthens all the major muscle groups in the body and exercises the respiratory system. Each position balances with the one before, stretching the body in a different way and alternately expanding and contracting the chest to regulate the breathing.*

From www.yogaeverywhere.com

Two Sun Salutations each day will take 5 minutes, which is a small investment of time for a big return in quality of life.

Start with an easy walking warm-up.

### Sun Salutation

1. **Mountain.** Begin by standing comfortably erect with both feet firmly on the floor, shoulder width apart. Your hands are in front of your chest, palms together in a position of prayer.

2. **High 'C'.** Inhale and, as your lungs fill with air and your chest swells to a count of 3, bring your arms up and over your head in one fluid motion, keeping the palms of your hands together. Your head, neck and back follow the hands by arching gently as you exhale.

3. **Body Fold.** Go from extension to flexion by bending at the waist, dropping your head towards your knees and bringing your hands to your feet (or mat if you're flexible). If you can't get down to your feet allow the knees to bend until you can. Take one full inhalation and exhalation in this position.

*We shall not cease from exploration*
*And the end of all our exploring*
*Will be to arrive at where we started*
*And know the place for the first time.*

T. S. Elliot (Little Gidding)

4. **Step Back Lunge**.
   Your left leg bends at
   the knee as your right
   leg reaches back;
   you're maintaining a
   slight bend in the
   right knee. At the
   completion of this

   move, your left knee should be over the left foot and your head up
   and forward.

5. **Plank**. As you
   inhale, your left
   foot moves back to
   join the right foot
   and your hands
   remain on the floor.
   As the illustration
   shows, this plank

   position is like the beginning of a classic push-up. The designation
   'plank' comes from the fact that your body is held as straight as
   possible by contracting your abdominal muscles. This contraction
   can be enhanced as you exhale.

6. **Table Top**. Breathe
   in and drop your
   knees to the mat, so
   you are in a kneeling
   position with a flat
   (table top) back.

7. **Child's Pose**. Allow
   your butt to sink back
   on your heels. Your
   hands slide forward
   on the mat until they
   are outstretched with
   the forehead touching
   the floor between
   your arms.

**Yoga Levity**

*My yoga instructor upset me, so I offered him my special "moon salutation".*

Anonymous

*Flip 'yoga' backwards, throw in an 'n' and you've got 'agony'.*

Anonymous

*A dyslexic cow obtained spiritual enlightenment by going 'OOOOMMMM'.*

Again, no one will own up to this.

8. **The Stretching Cat.** Your hands stay flat on the mat as your head glides forward and your elbows start to bend. Your back arches upward, bringing your butt up from the heels.
Your head stays down with eyes looking into the mat.

9. **The Hooded Cobra.** This is a beautiful extension. Bring your chest down to the mat and unhook your toes. Slide your legs back until your thighs touch the mat.
Breathe in and slowly raise your head and neck up and back. Push down on your hands and straighten your arms to assist the smooth arching of your back from the waist. Don't force the extension and don't lock your arms. Breathe out.

10. **Downward Dog.** The yoga move we all seem to know. Feet, legs, arms and hips combine to elevate the butt until you have attained an inverted 'V' position. Your arms and legs straighten and you try
to elongate everything from your shoulders to your hands and from your butt to your feet. Push your heels towards the mat and hold the position for one complete inhalation/exhalation.

**The Fourfold Way: Walking the Paths of the Warrior, Teacher, Healer and Visionary**

By Angeles Arien

The Fourfold Way can by viewed as a formula for living well in whatever circumstance or culture you find yourself. It is a book of practical wisdom.

1. Show-up to whatever is in your path.
2. Pay attention to what has heart and meaning for you (personal rituals; things which sustain you).
3. Be true to yourself. (Be aware of your instincts and beliefs.)
4. Let go of expected outcomes. (Very important, but so hard to do).

*Long I stood and watched the trees*
*Wishing I were wise as these*
*For the hardest thing to know*
*Is the art and grace of letting go.*

From the poem *Letting Go*
by Jamie Sexton Holmes

11. **Step Forward Lunge**. Inhale, bend your right knee and bring your right foot forward until it's beside your hands. This is the mirror image of the  Step Back Lunge with the right knee over the right foot. Your left leg is stretched back, slightly bent at the knee, toes curled under. Breathe out and drop your hips a little to stretch out the quads.

12. **Body Fold**. Breathe in and bring your left foot forward until your feet are together. As in the previous Body Fold try to keep the hands on the mat, even if you have to bend your knees. Drop your head between your arms to knee level and exhale.

13. **Roll Up, Roll Up**. With your knees slightly bent, breathe in, keeping your butt tight and arms loose, roll up one vertebra at a time.

*Yoga, before you've practiced, the theory is useless. After you've practiced, the theory is obvious.*

David Williams

*Yoga is invigoration in relaxation. Freedom in routine. Confidence through self control. Energy within and energy without.*

Ymber Delecto

14. **High 'C'.** As before, inhale and bring your arms overhead with palms together. Your head, neck and spine arch back allowing the chest to rise as you breathe out.

15. **Mountain.** Keep your palms together as your elbows bend to allow your hands to assume the prayer position. The head, neck and back straighten until they are in a relaxed, erect posture. For the last 15 seconds take a deep breath for a count of four. Hold the breath for 5 seconds and exhale for 6 seconds.

Pause and repeat the Sun Salutation once more, this time using your opposite limbs so that your left leg extends back in the Step Back Lunge.

Note: If yoga is not your style, that's fine, but try to find some routine to challenge all the major muscles in your body.

If you wish to pursue breath control and meditation more deeply, the following CD will be a rewarding next step.

**CALM DOWN**

A series of breath-centered meditations by Nancy Wardle, MD

Dr. Wardle writes,
Calm Down *is a series of guided meditations and relaxation exercises that use various mind/body breath techniques. Over the past twenty years, in private practice and in workshops, they have been used successfully with my patients dealing with medical crisis and other clients who needed to build their stress resiliency.*

Tracks on *Calm Down* range from the 5-minute *Letting Go Breath* to the 21-minute deep relaxation from which the CD took its title, *Calm Down.*

This CD provides a pathway to the, *Still, small voice of calm,* which we all need to hear.

*Calm Down* can be purchased through Speakwell at www.speakwell.com. Just click on the WellMart button or call 1-866-721-6940 toll free.

*The single, most effective relaxation technique I know is conscious regulation of the breath.*

Andrew Weil

# The Power of Fifteen – Part 3

### 15 Breaths

The body and mind are one and the only way to separate them is with a guillotine. When we are tense and stressed our breathing tends to be shallow and fast. If we breathe deeply, slowly and rhythmically the body/mind is given the message that all is well and that we can relax. The relaxation that just a few breaths bring is profound and resonates throughout the body/mind. There is a decrease in circulating cortisol, adrenaline and glucocorticosteroids, all of which drive the stress response. Brain waves shift from the rapid Beta cycles to a slower Alpha/Theta state. Heart rate slows, blood pressure drops and muscle tension decreases. Instead of being in a hair-trigger reactive state, we move into an easy responsive state. All those beneficial changes are just a few breaths away.

### The Fifteen Breaths

Settle down, take you time and allow yourself to be in the moment. Don't just do something, sit there. Begin with an exhalation through the mouth that gently empties your lungs while contracting your belly. Pause a second and then inhale through the nose. Feel the lungs and belly expand as you fill the lungs completely. Pause briefly and then begin the next breath cycle with an exhalation.

As you breathe, try to stay in the moment without allowing the mind to

*An unhurried sense of time is itself a form of wealth.*

Bonnie Friedman

*And now I see with eye serene, the very pulse of the machine: A being breathing thoughtful breath, A traveler betwixt life and death.*

Wordsworth

*Sooner or later every one of us breathes an atom that has been breathed before by anyone you can think of who has lived before us – Michelangelo or George Washington or Moses.*

Jacob Bronowski

wander into the past or future. As thoughts enter your mind acknowledge them, and let them go. (The Buddhists refer to the constant chatter in your head as *monkey mind*). You will find that closing your eyes is helpful as it removes a number of visual stimuli. Like all things, this simple form of breath-centered meditation takes practice. We are not used to clearing our mind, focusing on the miracle of our breath and *falling awake*.

If only more physicians would prescribe deep breathing instead of tranquillizers, we would have a more relaxed and less drug dependent society. But people have been conditioned to want a pill prescription, rather than finding their own way to peace and tranquility.

You can use the 15 breaths any time you feel stressed or pressured and it will take you 3 to 4 minutes. You can structure them as part of your day, along with walking and the Sun Salutation. If you're at work and time is pressing, even 5 breaths will start moving you out of a reactive, adrenal driven state and into a calmer space.

### The Power of 15 Rx

Exhale through the mouth for a count of 6, trying to empty your lungs by contracting your belly. Pause and then inhale through the nose for a count of 5. Hold for 4 seconds and repeat until you have completed 15 breath cycles, each of about 15 seconds.

When you inhale, make sure you fill your lungs down to the bottom. The bottom part of the lungs is richly supplied with blood vessels, making it easy for the body to take up oxygen and get rid of carbon dioxide. Another word for breathing is *inspire*, and it is useful to think of breathing as *inspiration* where you take in good things. Think of breathing out as a letting go or releasing problems and stressors in your life.

As I sit here writing, and as you sit there reading, our breath is doing what it knows how to do, bringing oxygen into the body and releasing carbon dioxide that the body does not need. A constant miracle, the breath is our moment to moment reminder of being and it is the source of essential energy for every cellular function.

*Life is not measured by the number
of breaths we take, but by the moments
that take our breath away.*

George Carlin

---

**We are indeed walking miracles.**

Early in the book I said that you were a *walking miracle*. The lungs are just one more example of the miraculous design and engineering of the human body. If you were able to spread your lungs out their surface area would be similar to that of a regulation tennis court. Yet they are folded and contoured so exquisitely that they fit comfortably in our chest.

---

We are rarely conscious of our breath, it does its job without our having to pay attention. Yet it is in the act of paying attention, when we choose to, that affords the possibility of using the breath to restore balance in the face of life's constant demands and disruptions. By being mindful of breath, especially by recognizing the importance of exhaling completely to allow for full inhalation, we give the mind and body an opportunity to integrate and marshal its resources and to connect with our be-ingness rather than our constant do-ingness.

### Summary
## The Power of Fifteen
## Weight Loss Phase

1. 15000 steps per day
   1500 calories per day for guaranteed weight loss and cardiovascular conditioning.
2. The 15-part Sun Salutation for overall body conditioning.
3. Fifteen 15-second breaths for balancing and relaxation.

## The Power of Fifteen
## Weight Maintenance

1. 45 – 60 minutes of purposeful walking.
   You can think in terms of 3 x 15-minute or 4 x 15 minute walks. 1500 quality calories, plus some of your own favorite foods that might not fit in a 1500-calorie formula.
2. Daily 15-part Sun Salutation.
   Plus additional strength and flexibility work.
3. Fifteen 15-second focused breaths for balancing and letting go.

Walking, stretching, eating well and breathing, it all seems so simple, and maybe it is. Dr. Albert Schweitzer told us that, *From naïve simplicity, we arrive at a more profound simplicity.*

## *Be Well*

*A merry heart maketh like good medicine.*

Proverbs 15-13

*Enjoy every sandwich.*

Warren Zevon

*I finally figured out the reason to be alive is to enjoy it.*

Rita Mae Brown

# Appendix:

# Screening and Testing

## The birth of the Physical Activity Readiness Questionnaire (PAR-Q)

Do you need a screening test before starting a walking program? Probably not. However, if you are very overweight, have pre-existing conditions such as high blood pressure, diabetes, heart problems or muscular skeletal injuries it is useful to consult a physician. The people who really need a screening test are those who propose to do absolutely no exercise, as this is far more dangerous to the human body than walking.

Thirty years ago the Canadian Government created the Canadian Home Fitness Test, which was a step test to determine cardiovascular fitness. However, they were concerned that someone might have an adverse medical response doing the test and that the government would be held liable. I and three colleagues were given the task of creating a screening test to see if people could safely start an exercise program, or step test, or whether they should check with a doctor first. We tested over twelve hundred people who first responded to a battery of over 30 questions and were then given an extensive medical and physiological evaluation, including a monitored stress test. The answers on the questionnaire were correlated with their testing results to find out which questions were important in identifying people who might be at risk

*It's the sides of the mountain, not the top that
sustain life.*

Pirsig

*If you refuse to accept nothing but the best, it's
surprising how often you get it.*

Unknown

*No one can make you feel inferior without your
consent.*

Eleanor Roosevelt

starting an exercise program.

This piece of research gave birth to PAR-Q (Physical Activity Readiness Questionnaire), which, with some minor modifications, is used throughout the Western World today. The version I'm including was revised in 2002 and used in the book, "Steps to Better Health" published by the Cooper Institute with whom I have cooperated over the years. It is still a 7-item questionnaire and 6 of the 7 questions are the same as the original with some clarification of the wording.

If you are planning a significant increase in your physical activity and are between the ages of 15 and 69 PAR-Q will tell you if it is advisable to see a doctor before you start. If you are in the 70+ age group it's a good idea to check with your doctor anyway. Common sense and honesty are your guides when checking these questions *yes* or *no*.

## YES   NO

| | | |
|---|---|---|
| | | Has your doctor ever said that you have a heart condition and that you should only do physical activity recommended by a doctor? |
| | | Do you feel pain in your chest when you do physical activity? |
| | | In the past month, have you had chest pain when you were not doing physical activity? |
| | | Do you lose your balance because of dizziness or do you ever lose consciousness? |
| | | Do you have a bone or joint problem (for example, back, knee, or hip) that could be made worse by a change in your physical activity? |
| | | Is your doctor currently prescribing drugs (for example, water pills) for your blood pressure or heart condition? |

*Exercise deficiency – the sweat deficit – is a self-inflicted disease. Our tendency is to cheat on ourselves. We think we can enjoy the fullness of life without paying for it. But that is not the way the world works – or the human machine either; Nothing is free.*

George Sheehan

*Tears will get you sympathy, sweat will get you change.*

Jesse Jackson

<u>**YES**</u>  <u>**NO**</u>

| | | |
|---|---|---|
| | | Do you know of any other reason why you should not do physical activity? |

The research team for the original PAR-Q comprised D. Chisholm, MD, L Kulak, MD, G. Stewart, MS and M. Collis, PhD

Another formula, which came out of this research, was from an article I wrote for the BC Medical Journal Vol. 16, #9, September 1974. To help doctors prescribe exercise for their patients I created the FITT acronym, standing for Frequency, Intensity, Time and Type. Like PAR-Q, this is still widely used today. For a walking program this might look like:

**Frequency:** Daily

**Intensity:** This can be measured by heart rate. For beginners, stay with the lower 'Fit Start' heart rate initially, but as you increase the speed and distance of your walking move into a 'Keep Fit' heart rate zone.

| Fit Start | | Keep Fit | |
|---|---|---|---|
| Age | Heart Rate | Age | Heart Rate |
| 20 – 29 | 118 | 20 – 29 | 146 – 164 |
| 30 – 39 | 112 | 30 – 39 | 138 – 156 |
| 40 – 49 | 106 | 40 – 49 | 130 – 148 |
| 50 – 59 | 100 | 50 – 59 | 122 – 140 |
| 60 – 69 | 94 | 60 – 69 | 116 - 132 |

**Time:**  45 minutes continuous.

**Type:**  Walking at 3 1/2mph (5.6kph) or for someone else it might be Power Walking at 5mph (8kph).

### Personal Fitness Test

It is interesting and motivational to test your walking performance and

*May you grow up to be righteous*
*May you grow up to be swift*
*May you have a strong foundation*
*When the winds of changes shift*
*May you build a ladder to the stars*
*And climb on every rung*
*May you stay forever young.*

Bob Dylan

predicted maximal oxygen uptake on a simple standardized test. The *Rockport Fitness Walking Test* is available free of charge on the web and involves access to a 400-meter track and the use of a stopwatch.

### Treadmill Walking Test

A number of the higher end treadmills have fitness testing programs built into the programming. An example of this is the Tunturi 2km-walking test with the fitness index based on time to complete the 2km walk and your heart rate at the end of the session.

There are other forms of tests including testing for muscle strength and endurance, flexibility, body composition and many, many more. The key to a successful lifestyle change however, is not whether you're tested, but whether you follow a program of exercise and good nutrition.

*The big secret in life is that there is no big secret.*
*Whatever your goal, you can probably reach it if*
*you are willing to work.*

Oprah Winfrey

*I could have missed the pain*
*But I'd have had to miss the dance.*

Tony Arata *The Dance*
Sung by Garth Brooks

### Get a good price on a good pedometer

Enclose this coupon to save $4.00 on each Speakwell H215 pedometer you order up to a limit of 10 pedometers (regular price $19 each CAD).

| | |
|---|---|
| Canadian price | $15.00/each |
| US price | $13.50/each |

Shipping and Handling is $8.00 for the first pedometer and $2.00 for each additional unit, up to a maximum of 10 pedometers.

| | |
|---|---|
| I wish to order _____ (#) of Speakwell H215 pedometer(s) (maximum 10) at $15 each ($13.50 US)                    Pedometer  Total Cost | |
| Shipping and Handling $8 for first pedometer, $2 for each additional unit. | |
| GST 6% (Canadian residents only on total of pedometers plus shipping and handling fee). | |
| PST 7% (BC residents only on total $ of pedometers **not** on shipping and handling charge) | |
| Total | |

Mail this page and include your name, full mailing address and phone number along with a cheque for the total made out to *Speakwell* to:

Speakwell
2572 Arbutus Rd.
Victoria, BC V8N 1W2
Canada

If you would like your order charged to your Visa or MasterCard please fill out the following:

Name on the credit card: _____

Credit Card Number: _____

Expiry Date: _____     Visa ❑     MasterCard ❑

If you have any questions please call 866-721-6940 toll-free.

I wish to thank the people who've helped me, healed me, inspired me and befriended me and on whose shoulders I've stood to look over the fence of my own limitations.

Bob Allen, Judd Allen, Norma Alison, Kare Anderson, Don Ardell, Dino Asproloupos, Lee Beames, Lynne Beecroft, Rick Bell, Sherry Bell, Kendy Bentley, Steven Blair, John Boehme, Dominique Boltres, Shane Brown, Peter Buitenhuis, Colin Campbell, Tony Casey, Art Charlton, Dave Chisholm, Monte Clark, Diane Clement, Doug Clement, Betty Collis, Eric Collis, Joan Collis, Ken Cooper, Mel Cooper, Ann Cowan, Rhonda Cox, Cheryl Craver, Wally Craver, Tony Davies, Ray Davies, Janice Dillon, Ian Dixon , Dave Docherty, Catherine Dore, Phillip Dore, Dave Dummer, Celia Duthie, Rob Dyke, Bob Dylan, Mark Fenton, Jane Fernyhough, Mike Fleet, Rich Gafter-Ricks, Kathy Gaul, Gwyn Gardom, Sandy Gibbons, Wynn Gmitroski, George Haines, Carol Handford, Murray Handford, Geoff Harris, Kelty Harris, Rob Hasegawa, Joe Henderson, Tim Herperger, Bill Hettler, Ryan Heumann, James Hill, Richard Hills, Art Hister, Nick Hornby, Diana Ingram, Bonnie Ireland, Simon Ibell, David Iles, Deb Jones, Sandy Keir, Steve King, Bill Kinsella, Russ Kisby,, Claudia Kolb-Thomas, Tim Lane, Silken Laumann, Lara Lauzon, Bob Lawrence, Guy le Mesurier, Susan Lee, Linda Lewis-Daly, Marie MacDonald, Doug Manson-Blair, George Marsden, Penny Marsden, Veronica Marsden, Lois Mason, Peter Mason, Jim McAvoy, Connie McAvoy, Katz McCarthy, Don McCarthy, Ross McKay, Neil McKinlay, Beth McKinney, James McLaren, Gord Medd, Lauve Metcalf, Errol Miller, Gord Miller, Linda Miller, Belinda Miller-Foey, Jef Moonen, Murph the Surf, Jean Nash, John Nash, Steve Nash, P J Naylor, Doug Nichols, Lindsay Niedjalski, Luke Niedjalski, Ron Nye, Eileen O'Byrne, Mary Jane O'Byrne, Lorenzo Oss-Cech, Johanne Paquette, Andre Picard, Miles Primrose, Wylie Rauch, Naz Rayani, Rob Reid, Tom Reid, Judy Reynolds, Jennifer Richardson, Jackie Riley, Art Salmon, Ian Scanlon, Dave Secco, Debbie Secco, George Sheehan, Kathy Shields, Ken Shields, Doug Sims, Nancy Singleton, Barbara Skillings, Roger Skillings, Trina Sporer, Ben Sporer, Charles Sterling, Susan Sterling, Gord Stewart, Marty Stone, Jill Tait, Joe Taylor, Jane Thom, Mark Tremblay, Christine Truscott, Catrine Tudor-Locke, Frank Van Gyn, Geri Van Gyn, Gus Verstraten, Kathy Vinton, Randy Voldeng, Sandy Voldeng, John Wardle, Pat Wardle, Howie Wenger, Joan Wharf-Higgins, Johathan Willcocks, Claire Winfield, Bobbe Wood, Warren Zevon, The Escargots, Logan Lake Wellness Centre, Trainload of Fools, All the Parkside staff, Crystal Palace F.C. and many colleagues at the University of Victoria.

If I've overlooked a good friend, please let me know.

The group of people who complete my happiness are my two children, Christy and Paul, their spouses, Sue and Karen and their three children, Sasha, Toby and Holly. All seven are vegetarians, which shows how little impact I had on their eating style. The world is a better place for these seven people and a big part of my wellness plan is to enjoy time with them for years to come

I wondered what a list of all the people who have had a real negative impact on my life would look like. I couldn't think of one name to start the list. Well, well, well.

Dr. Martin Collis

Martin has a rich and interesting background and the many strands from his academic and professional career have been woven together to create *Walking, Weight and Wellness*. He has a Ph.D. in exercise physiology from Stanford University and, while in California, also coached swimming and worked with many Olympic medal winners and world record holders.

He wrote the first North American book on *Employee Fitness* and the Canadian Government's weight management book, *The Phacts of Life*. He was the co-creator of PAR-Q (Physical Activity Readiness Questionnaire), which is widely used as a screening tool for people entering exercise programs. Martin represented the *President's Council on Physical Fitness* to promote workplace wellness throughout the USA and his contributions have been recognized by the White House and the Prime Minister of Canada.

Currently his passion is to promote physical activity and lifestyle artistry throughout North America. He does this as a highly entertaining keynote speaker, through his online webzine, *Well*, as a singer/songwriter with a recorded repertoire of wellness related songs, as a promoter of worksite walking and wellness and now with *Walking, Weight and Wellness*.

Martin currently resides in Victoria, BC with his wife Nancy and their cat, Susie. He is ever mindful of the words of Marianne Moore that, *to miss the joy is to miss it all.*

Printed in the United Kingdom
by Lightning Source UK Ltd.
135412UK00001B/177/A